CAMPAIGN • 208

PETERSBURG 1864–65

The longest siege

RON FIELD

ILLUSTRATED BY PETER DENNIS

Series editors Marcus Cowper and Nikolai Bogdanovic

First published in 2009 by Osprey Publishing
Midland House, West Way, Botley, Oxford OX2 0PH, UK
443 Park Avenue South, New York, NY 10016, USA
E-mail: info@ospreypublishing.com

ISBN 978-184603-355-1
PDF e-book ISBN: 978 1 84603 886 0

Editorial by Ilios Publishing Ltd, Oxford, UK (www.iliospublishing.com)
Design: The Black Spot
Cartography: Bounford.com
Bird's-eye view artworks: The Black Spot
Index by Margaret Vaudrey
Originated by United Graphic Pte Ltd, Singapore

09 10 11 12 13   10 9 8 7 6 5 4 3 2 1

A CIP catalog record for this book is available from the British Library.

FOR A CATALOG OF ALL BOOKS PUBLISHED BY OSPREY MILITARY AND AVIATION PLEASE CONTACT:

NORTH AMERICA
Osprey Direct, c/o Random House Distribution Center, 400 Hahn Road, Westminster, MD 21157
E-mail: uscustomerservice@ospreypublishing.com

ALL OTHER REGIONS
Osprey Direct, The Book Service Ltd, Distribution Centre, Colchester Road, Frating Green, Colchester, Essex, CO7 7DW
E-mail: customerservice@ospreypublishing.com

www.ospreypublishing.com

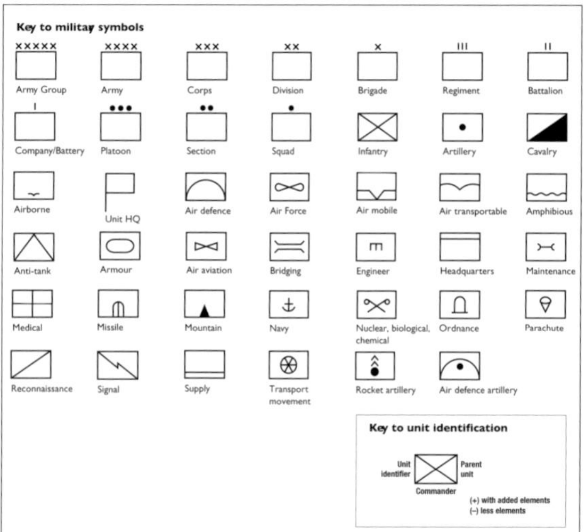

DEDICATION

For my friends Mary and Rick Hatcher.

ARTIST'S NOTE

Readers may care to note that the original paintings from which the color plates in this book were prepared are available for private sale. The Publishers retain all reproduction copyright whatsoever. All enquiries should be addressed to:

Peter Dennis,
Fieldhead,
The Park,
Mansfield,
Nottinghamshire
NG18 2AT, UK

The Publishers regret that they can enter into no correspondence upon this matter.

THE WOODLAND TRUST

Osprey Publishing are supporting the Woodland Trust, the UK's leading woodland conservation charity, by funding the dedication of trees.

CONTENTS

An overview of the Petersburg campaign, June 1864–April 1865 (see notes opposite)

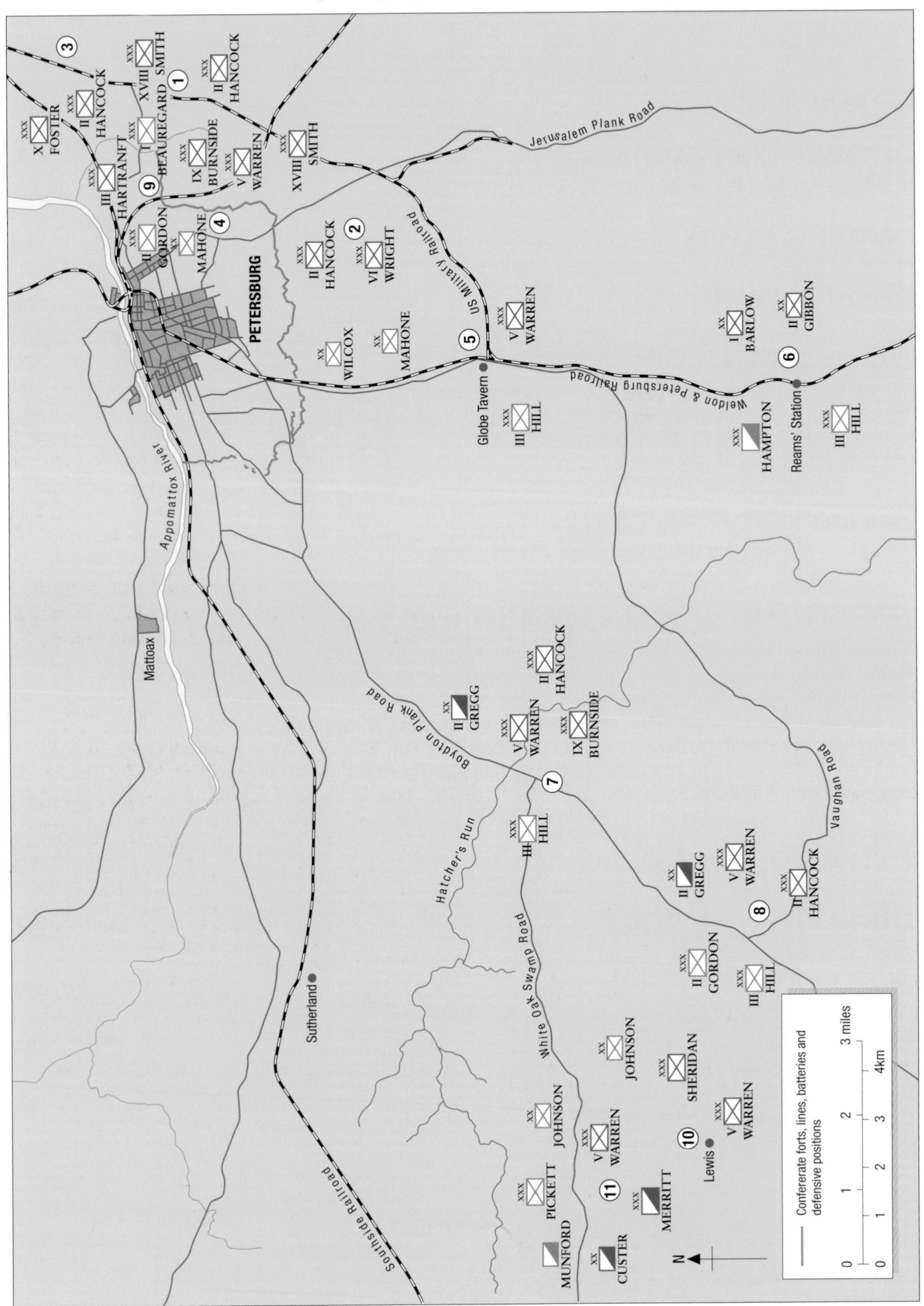

INTRODUCTION

With the foresight of a military genius, Robert E. Lee met with General Jubal Early at the beginning of June 1864, and advised him that the Confederate forces must at all costs "destroy this Army of Grant's before it gets to [the] James River, if he gets there it will become a siege and then it will be a mere question of time." The events of the following months, beginning with the sequence of slaughter known as the "Overland Campaign" involving battles at the Wilderness, Spotsylvania Court House, North Anna and Cold Harbor, and ending with the final breaking of the siege of Petersburg on April 2, 1865, were to prove how right he was.

Earlier in 1862, at the commencement of his Tennessee River campaign, General Ulysses S. Grant had commented to army surgeon Major John Hill Brinton, "The art of war is simple enough. Find out where your enemy is.

1 June 15, 1864. The Union XVIII Corps arrives and breaks through the eastern end of the Dimmock Line forcing the Confederates to withdraw to a temporary secondary line along Harrison's Creek. Although reinforced by the II Corps, Smith fails to follow up his success. Following two more days of fighting, during which more of the southern section of the Dimmock falls, the Confederates withdraw from Harrison's Creek to inner defense works, and the siege begins.

2 June 21, 1864. The Union II Corps, supported by the VI Corps, attempts to cut the Weldon Railroad. Lee retaliates the next day by counterattacking with Willcox's and Mahone's divisions of Hill's III Corps, which forces the II Corps back to the Jerusalem Plank Road, where they dig in.

3 July 27, 1864. Elements of the Union X Corps, reinforced by the II Corps, cross the James River at Deep Bottom to attack the Richmond defenses, which diverts part of the Confederate force defending Richmond. Realizing the potential of this tactic, Grant uses it on two further occasions.

4 June 25, 1864. The Petersburg mining operation begins. On July 30 the mine is detonated under Elliott's Salient. The Union IX Corps, supported by elements of the V and XVIII Corps, fails to break through the Confederate lines, and many of its men are trapped and killed, wounded or captured in the Crater during a Confederate counterattack led by Mahone.

5 August 18, 1864. The Union V Corps mounts a second attempt to cut the Weldon Railroad. Griffin's division destroys the tracks while Ayres' Division, supported by Crawford's Division, holds off a Confederate counterattack. Hill's III Corps counterattacks the next day and the V Corps withdraws to Globe Tavern and digs in. Lee is repulsed and loses control of the upper part of the Weldon Railroad.

6 August 21, 1864. The Union 1st and 2nd divisions, II Corps continue the destruction of the lower part of the Weldon Railroad near Reams' Station. The next day, the Confederate III Corps plus Wade Hampton's cavalry attack and break through the faulty Union earthworks, forcing Hancock to withdraw by the end of the day.

7 September 30, 1864. Elements of the Union V and IX Corps, plus Gregg's cavalry, advance westward to cut the Boydton Plank Road and Southside Railroad, and attack Confederate earthworks at Peebles' Farm. Hill counterattacks and drives them back to Pegram's Farm. A Confederate flanking attack along Squirrel Level Road is repulsed the next day. Reinforced by elements of the II Corps, Union forces continue to advance on October 2 and extend the Union lines to Peebles' and Pegram's farms. The II, V, and IX Corps, plus Gregg's cavalry division, capture the Boydton Plank Road on October 27–28, but a Confederate counterattack by Heth's Division and Hampton's cavalry near Burgess' Mill isolates the II Corps and forces a retreat. The Confederates retain control of the Boydton Plank Road for the rest of the winter.

8 February 5, 1865. Gregg's cavalry, shielded by the V and II Corps, attempt to capture the Boydton Plank Road, but are repulsed by elements of Gordon's II Corps and Hill's III Corps at the Battle of Hatcher's Run. Union forces dig in and extend their siege lines to the Vaughan Road.

9 March 25, 1865. Attempting a breakout of the siege lines, Gordon's corps attacks Fort Stedman but is repulsed by a Union counterattack organized by Hartranft's 3rd Division, IX Corps.

10 March 29 and 31, 1865. Sheridan's cavalry and the V Corps seize control of the Boydton Plank Road and force the Confederates under Bushrod Johnson back to the White Oak Swamp Road. Pickett's Corps is isolated and forced to withdraw, leaving the Southside Railroad undefended.

11 April 1, 1865. Sheridan defeats Pickett at Five Forks and captures the Southside Railroad. Grant orders an advance along the whole front, and Petersburg falls the next day.

The gallant defense of the small garrison at an unfinished Confederate earthwork called Fort Gregg bought the time Robert E. Lee needed in order to conduct a withdrawal from Petersburg and Richmond during the night of April 2–3, 1865. Serving one of the guns, a Confederate cannoneer is shown pulling the lanyard as Union troops storm over the breastworks at the moment the fort fell. (Courtesy of the National Park Service)

Get at him as soon as you can. Strike him as hard as you can, and keep moving on." At forts Henry and Donelson, Vicksburg and Chattanooga, Grant demonstrated the effectiveness of this approach to warfare. Once appointed general-in-chief of all the Union armies on March 12, 1864, based on his success in the western theater of war, he had the opportunity to put this philosophy into action on the grand scale in order to achieve the final defeat of the Confederacy.

On taking command, Grant's plan was simple. With a determination to use the greater manpower of the Northern States, he called for a "simultaneous movement all along the line," and advised Major General George G. Meade, commanding the 115,000-strong Army of the Potomac, "Lee's army will be your objective point. Wherever Lee goes, there you will go also." In conjunction with this, the Western army, now commanded by General William Tecumseh Sherman, was ordered to capture Atlanta in Georgia, and then "get into the interior of the enemy's country" to inflict as much damage as possible. Meanwhile, the 30,000-strong army under Nathaniel Banks would capture Mobile in Alabama. An army of equal size under Benjamin F. Butler would advance up the peninsula in Virginia to threaten Richmond, and Franz Sigel's command of 26,000 men would invade the Shenandoah Valley to destroy the "breadbasket" of the Confederacy. However, Grant's 1864 strategy did not all go according to plan. Although Sherman achieved remarkable success by capturing Savannah, Georgia, Banks was defeated in the Red River Campaign, Butler failed in his attempt to approach Richmond, and Sigel was defeated in the valley. Much seemed to hinge on the success of the campaign in Northern Virginia.

Accompanying the Army of the Potomac, commanded by Major General George G. Meade, Grant conducted a relentless pounding of Lee's army in a costly campaign of attrition through the battles of the Wilderness, Spotsylvania Court House, North Anna and Cold Harbor. Crossing the Rapidan River on May 4, he halted his large army of approximately 107,500 men for the night in the Wilderness near Spotsylvania Court House. The next day, Lee surprised him in the two-day indecisive battle of the Wilderness, which cost 18,000 Union and 11,000 Confederate casualties.

Farther south, most of Butler's 33,000 Union soldiers in the X and XVIII Corps, Army of the James, advanced up the James River on May 5, in a combined army–navy fleet of 120 transports, gunboats, ironclads and assorted vessels, in an additional attempt to close in on Richmond. Seizing Wilson's Wharf and Fort Powhatan, seven miles upriver, and City Point a further 12 miles closer to the Confederate capital, his forces advanced into Bermuda Hundred, but were prevented from progressing further by strong Confederate fortifications. Constructing his own defenses, Butler launched an unsuccessful attempt to capture Drewry's Bluff on May 12, the failure of which he blamed on Major General Quincy Adams Gillmore.

Meanwhile, in an attempt to draw the Confederates out of the Wilderness, Grant headed southeast toward Spotsylvania Court House, but part of Lee's forces arrived there first. On May 8 the battle of Spotsylvania began, culminating in brutal hand-to-hand combat in the Confederate earthworks at a point subsequently called the "Bloody Angle." After a repulse by Confederate artillery on May 18, Grant marched his vast army east and south. However, Lee forced the Union army apart at North Anna Creek by deploying his own force in an inverted "V," and on May 26, as Grant advanced toward Richmond, Lee formed a strong defensive line along Totopotomoy Creek. On May 30 Lee attacked part of Grant's army near Bethesda Church, and on June 1 the armies clashed in the battle of Cold Harbor. Three days later Grant launched a frontal attack to break Lee's line, but was repulsed with 12,000 Union soldiers killed or wounded. Strategically the "Overland Campaign," which ended after the slaughter at Cold Harbor, was a Union success as Grant's army was only about six miles from Richmond. But it had cost 60,000 Union casualties, plus perhaps 35,000 Confederate losses, and Richmond was still in Confederate hands.

Having failed to break through at Cold Harbor on June 4, Grant decided to change his strategy. Instead of confronting and defeating Lee's army in the open north of Richmond, he decided to capture the Confederate capital by crossing the James River and approaching it from the south. By cutting the Confederate supply lines and capturing Petersburg with his larger army and superior resources, he believed he could either starve Lee's Army of Northern Virginia into submission or lure them away from Richmond for a decisive battle.

Although the campaign that followed involved nine and one-half months of siege warfare, which represents the longest siege in American military history, it also consisted of a series of six major battles, 11 engagements, 50 skirmishes, six assaults and four expeditions, as Union forces at first tried to capture Petersburg in an all-out attack, and then concentrated on seizing the various road and rail supply routes south of the city that formed the lifeline of the Confederate capital.

OPPOSING COMMANDERS

A member of a prominent Virginia family, Robert E. Lee was born at Stafford Hall, Virginia, in 1807 and graduated from West Point second in a class of 46 in 1829. Serving in the Corps of Engineers, he emerged from the Mexican-American War with one wound, three brevets for bravery, and a brilliant reputation. He was superintendent at West Point from 1852 to 1855. In Washington, DC when the John Brown raid at Harpers Ferry occurred in October 1859, he was sent to put down that insurrection. He opposed the secession of his home state, but rejected President Lincoln's offer to command the Union forces. When Virginia seceded from the Union in April 17, 1861, Lee resigned from the US Army and accepted the command of the Virginia state forces. (Library of Congress LC-B8172-0001)

CONFEDERATE

Rejecting an offer from Lincoln to command the Union forces, **Robert E. Lee** resigned his commission in April 1861, holding the rank of colonel in the 1st Cavalry. Following his home state out of the Union on April 17, 1861, he accepted command of the Virginia State Forces with rank of major general, and served as senior military advisor to President Jefferson Davis. His first field command for the Confederate States (CS) came in June 1862 when he took command of Confederate forces in the Eastern Theater, which he renamed the Army of Northern Virginia. While he was responsible for Confederate victories at the Seven Days Battles, Second Bull Run, Fredericksburg and Chancellorsville, both his campaigns to invade the North ended in failure. He barely escaped defeat at Sharpsburg, or Antietam, in September 1862, and was decisively defeated during the third day at Gettysburg in July 1863, although Meade permitted him to withdraw back into Virginia. When Grant began his Overland Campaign on May 4, 1864, Lee's forces inflicted heavy casualties on the larger Union army, particularly at Cold Harbor, although Lee was unable to replace his own losses. Lee took command of the Petersburg defenses in June 1864. He was promoted to general-in-chief of Confederate forces on January 31, 1865.

Resigning from his post as superintendent of West Point five days after the secession of his home state of Louisiana, **P.G.T. Beauregard** was commissioned a brigadier general in the Confederate Army in March 1861, and was promoted to become one of the eight full generals in the Confederacy on July 21 of that year. His recommendation that strong forces should be stationed at New Orleans was rejected by Jefferson Davis, which resulted in a friction between the two men that would intensify as the Civil War progressed. He commanded the Confederate forces in Charleston Harbor that fired on Fort Sumter on April 12–13, 1861, and won the first main Confederate victory at Manassas, Virginia, in conjunction with General Joseph E. Johnston. Transferred to Tennessee in early 1862, he assumed command at Shiloh when General Albert Sidney Johnston was killed. He became sick in June of that year, and believed he had temporarily handed command to General Braxton Bragg while he went on leave. However, the Confederate president relieved him on the charge of abandoning his post without authority. Following recovery he returned to Charleston to take command of the defenses of the Carolina and Georgia coast, which he managed successfully until 1864 when he was ordered north to assist Robert E. Lee in the defense of Richmond and Petersburg.

LEFT
Pierre Gustave Toutant Beauregard was born at the "Contreras" plantation in St Bernard Parish near New Orleans in 1818. He became Superintendent of West Point in January, 1861, but resigned on February 20, 1861, and was at once appointed brigadier general in the CS Army. (US National Archives NWDNS-111-B-1239)

CENTER
Nicknamed "Little Billy" because of his diminutive stature, William Mahone was born in Virginia in 1826, the son of a tavern keeper. He graduated from the Virginia Military Institute with a degree as a civil engineer in the class of 1847. Pursuing a career in civil engineering, he was responsible for the construction of the Norfolk and Petersburg Railroad. His knowledge of the layout of the railroad system south of Petersburg would prove invaluable during the ensuing campaign, and in particular during the battle of the Jerusalem Plank Road, also known as First Weldon Railroad, on June 22, 1864. (US National Archives NWDNS-111-B-5123)

RIGHT
Of Scottish descent, John B. Gordon was born on his father's plantation in Upson County, Georgia, in 1832. Although an outstanding student, he failed to graduate from the University of Georgia, and moved to Atlanta where he became a qualified lawyer. Unable to prosper in this profession, he next moved to Milledgeville (then the state capital) where he became a journalist. Following this, he formed the Castle Rock Coal Company in partnership with his father, and at the outbreak of Civil War recruited the Racoon Roughs, Company I, 6th Alabama Infantry. (US National Archives NWDNS-111-B-1786)

Appointed quartermaster of Virginia forces upon secession, **William "Little Billy" Mahone** commanded the 6th Virginia Infantry during the capture of the Norfolk Navy Yard, and was appointed brigadier general of the Confederate States Army on November 16, 1861. He led his brigade at Seven Pines and Malvern Hill during the Peninsular Campaign of 1862, and was wounded at Second Bull Run later the same year. He recovered to fight at Fredericksburg, Chancellorsville, Gettysburg, the Wilderness, and Spotsylvania, and received an on-the-spot promotion to major general from Robert E. Lee following his repulse of Union forces during the Battle of the Crater on July 30, 1864.

John B. Gordon was elected major of the 6th Alabama Infantry on May 14, 1861. He received the colonelcy of that regiment on April 28, 1862. He succeeded the wounded General Robert E. Rodes in command of the First Brigade, Hill's Division of Jackson's Command, Army of Northern Virginia, during the Peninsular Campaign, and was wounded leading his unit at Sharpsburg on September 17, 1862. He was appointed brigadier general on November 1, 1862. As this was not confirmed, he was re-appointed during May 1863. He continued to command his brigade of Georgians at Chancellorsville, Gettysburg, the Wilderness and Spotsylvania, being named major general on May 14, 1864. Lee entrusted Gordon with command of the final attempt to break the siege of Petersburg, which resulted in the disastrous attack on Fort Stedman on March 25, 1865.

Returning east from his posting on San Juan Island, Washington Territory, **George Pickett** resigned his captaincy in the US Army on June 25, 1861, and assumed a commission as major in the CS artillery. Within a month he was appointed colonel in charge of the Rappahannock Line of the Department of Fredericksburg, under the command of Major General Theophilus H. Holmes. He was promoted to brigadier general on January 14, 1862, and commanded the 3rd Brigade of Longstreet's Division, nicknamed "The Gamecock Brigade," which he led at Williamsburg, Seven Pines and Gaines' Mill. He was wounded in the shoulder during the latter battle, but recovered and received promotion to major general on October 10, 1862, being placed in command of a division of Longstreet's corps. Holding the centre at Fredericksburg, his division saw little action from December 11 to 15, 1862, and was on detached service near Suffolk during the battle of Chancellorsville. He was immortalized in "Pickett's Charge" during the third day at Gettysburg, although he did not command the attack and the

Born in Richmond to a prominent Virginia family in 1825, George Edward Pickett studied law at Springfield, Illinois, and entered West Point at 17 years of age graduating in 1846 at the very bottom (known as "the goat") of a 59-man class. Commissioned a brevet second lieutenant in the 8th Infantry, he gained national recognition as the first American to climb the parapet during the Battle of Chapultepec in the Mexican-American War of 1846-48. Posted to Washington Territory, he commanded the construction of Fort Bellingham in 1856, and became involved in an international dispute with Great Britain when he occupied San Juan Island in 1859. Following the secession of his home state, he resigned from the army and journeyed back east to offer his services to the Confederacy. (Library of Congress DIG-cwpbh-00682)

Virginians of his division did not make up the largest part of the attacking force. His shattered division was sent to recuperate and recruit in the Department of Virginia and North Carolina on September 23, 1861, and he was appointed department commander. His attack on New Bern, North Carolina, in late January 1864 failed due to the poor performance of his subordinate, General Seth Barton. He next played a prominent role in the actions of General Benjamin Butler against Drewry's Bluff, Virginia, between May 4 and 16, 1864. His division rejoined the First Corps, Army of Northern Virginia, in time for Cold Harbor on June 1, and continued to serve under Lee throughout the Petersburg Campaign.

UNION

A regimental quartermaster with the rank of captain during the Mexican-American War of 1846–48, **Ulysses S. Grant** received two citations for gallantry and one for meritorious conduct. After the war he was unable to adapt to the monotony and isolation of military service on the West Coast and drank heavily, thereby neglecting his duty. As a result, he resigned from the army in 1854 to avoid court-martial, and settled in Missouri, where he became increasingly destitute as he failed to make a success of various business ventures. At the outbreak of the Civil War, he offered his services to Governor Richard Yates and trained recruits at Springfield, Illinois. Valued for his previous military experience, he accepted the colonelcy of the 21st Illinois Infantry in June 1861, and in August was appointed brigadier general of volunteers commanding the critical District of Southeast Missouri with headquarters at Cairo, Illinois. Following an unspectacular action against Belmont, Missouri on November 7, 1861, he gained national attention following his successful operations at forts Henry and Donelson, and Shiloh in 1862 and at Vicksburg in 1863. His willingness to fight and ability to win impressed President Lincoln, despite rumors of his continued inebriation. As a result, Grant was appointed general-in-chief of the Armies of the United States, with the rank of lieutenant general in the regular army, on March 12, 1864. Re-authorized by US Congress with Grant in mind, this rank had not been awarded since 1775 when George Washington was appointed commander-in-chief of the Continental Army, although Winfield Scott had received the brevet rank in 1855. Summoned east to Washington, DC, Grant planned and implemented the Overland Campaign to capture Richmond, Virginia, and ordered the investment of Petersburg in June 1864.

An artillery specialist, Captain **Quincy Adams Gillmore**, Corps of Engineers, was assigned to accompany General Thomas W. Sherman's expedition to Port Royal, South Carolina, in November 1861. He then took charge of siege operations against Fort Pulaski, Georgia, which concluded successfully with a Confederate surrender on April 11, 1862. Appointed brigadier general, he was ordered west to take command of the Second Division, Army of Kentucky. On July 10, 1863 he was appointed major general commanding the X Corps and Department of the South, consisting of North and South Carolina, Georgia and Florida, with headquarters at Hilton Head. He commanded forces that occupied Morris Island, Fort Wagner and Fort Gregg, and supervised the bombardment of Fort Sumter. However, he was unable to seize Charleston. On February 20, 1864 troops within his department were defeated at Olustee during the largest battle fought in Florida. In early May, 1864 the X Corps was transferred north to the Army of the James, in Virginia, where it took part in the Bermuda Hundred operations and also played an important role in the disastrous Drewry's Bluff action. Gillmore openly feuded with his superior officer, Major General Benjamin F. Butler, who held him responsible for the defeat. Nonetheless, as senior field officer he persuaded Butler at the last minute to let him lead the initial attack on Petersburg on June 9, 1863, replacing Brigadier General Edward Hincks, commanding the 3rd Brigade, XVIII Corps.

A captain in the Corps of Topographical Engineers before the Civil War, **George G. Meade** was promoted to brigadier general of volunteers on August 31, 1861, based on the strong recommendation of Pennsylvania's governor, Andrew Curtin. He was severely wounded at White Oak Swamp, one of the Seven Days Battles of 1862, but recovered sufficiently to take part in the Second Battle of Bull Run commanding a brigade of Pennsylvanians within Major General Irwin McDowell's III Corps of the Army of Virginia. His brigade made a heroic stand on Henry House Hill to protect the retreating Union Army, as a result of which he rose rapidly through the ranks, distinguishing himself during the Battle of South Mountain on September 14, 1862, commanding the 3rd Division, I Corps, Army of the Potomac. At Antietam four days later, Meade replaced the wounded Hooker in command of I Corps, but was again wounded. During the Union attack at Fredericksburg in December 1862, Meade's division achieved the only breakthrough on the Confederate lines, but he failed to reinforce his success leading to the loss of much of his division. Nonetheless he was promoted to major general of volunteers and received command of the V Corps, which he led at Chancellorsville during the spring of 1863. Meade replaced Hooker as commander of the Army of the Potomac on June 28, 1863. Just a few days later he fought and won a monumental victory at Gettysburg, although he was criticized by Lincoln and others for not aggressively pursuing the Confederates during their retreat. For the rest of 1863, in both the Bristoe and Mine Run campaigns, Meade was outmaneuvered by Lee. Reluctant to attack entrenched positions, he withdrew after fighting minor and inconclusive battles. When Grant was appointed commander of all Union armies in March 1864, Meade felt passed over and offered to resign. However, Grant refused to accept his resignation and established his headquarters with Meade, which caused additional friction between them for the remainder of the war.

Also a first lieutenant in the Topographical Corps at the start of war, **John G. Parke** was promoted to captain on September 9 and brigadier general of volunteers on November 23, 1861. Commanding the 3rd Brigade during Major General Ambrose Burnside's North Carolina expedition during early 1862, he fought at Roanoke Island, Fort Forrest, New Bern and Fort Macon. Later that year he led the 3rd Division, IX Corps, Army of the Potomac, at South Mountain and Antietam having been appointed major general on July 18, 1862. He next served as Burnside's chief of staff at Fredericksburg until January 25, 1863 when was appointed to command the IX Corps and ordered to join the Western Theatre for the Vicksburg campaign and defense of Knoxville. The IX Corps re-joined the Army of the Potomac in August 1863, and Parke became chief-of-staff to Burnside during the Overland Campaign. Replacing Burnside as corps commander after the failure of the assault on the Crater, he successfully assumed responsibility for rallying Union troops for a counterattack that prevented the Confederates from breaking through the siege lines at Fort Stedman on March 25, 1865.

At the commencement of war, Gouverneur **Kemble Warren** was a first

Born at Mount Pleasant, Ohio, on April 27, 1822, Ulysses Simpson Grant graduated from the United States Military Academy at West Point 21st out of a class of 39 in 1843. Although he was cited for bravery during the Mexican-American War of 1846–48, he languished during the 1850s, and would probably have been voted the man "least likely to succeed" in 1861. After a series of resounding victories in the Western Theater, he was ordered east by President Abraham Lincoln to become General-in-Chief of the Armies of the United States on March 12, 1864. He was photographed shortly after at Cold Harbor, Virginia, by the camera of Matthew Brady. (US National Archives NWDNS-111-B-36)

LEFT
Also a native of Ohio, Quincy Adams Gillmore was born at Black River in 1825. He received an appointment at West Point in 1845, and ranked first in his class when he graduated in 1849. Appointed to the Corps of Engineers, he helped plan the fortifications of Hampton Roads, Virginia, and in 1852 returned to West Point as an instructor of practical military engineering. During his years at the Academy, he studied the effects of cannon projectiles on masonry forts. In 1856, he transferred to New York City as chief army engineer in the region, and held this position at the outbreak of the Civil War. He commanded the initial Union attack on Petersburg on June 9, 1864, dubbed by the locals as the "battle of old men and young boys." (Library of Congress LC-B813-2239)

CENTER
George Gordon Meade was born in Spain of American parents in 1815 and graduated from West Point in 1835. He resigned a year later to become a civil engineer, but re-entered the army in 1842 and fought in the Mexican-American War, following which he served as a military engineer until the outbreak of Civil War. He would continue to command the Army of the Potomac after Grant became his superior in March, 1864. (US National Archives NWDNS-111-B-3298)

RIGHT
John Grubb Parke was born in Chester County, Pennsylvania, in 1827. He graduated from West Point in 1849 and was commissioned a second lieutenant in the Topographical Corps. In this capacity he determined the boundary lines between Iowa and the Little Colorado River, and was the chief surveyor of the party responsible for the delineation of the boundary of the northwest US and Canada from 1857 through 1861. (Library of Congress LC-BH831- 143)

lieutenant and mathematics instructor at West Point. He helped raise the 5th New York Infantry (Duryée's Zouaves) in May 1861, and was promoted to the colonelcy of that regiment following its participation at Big Bethel on June 10 of that year. He led the 5th New York at the Siege of Yorktown and assisted General A.A. Humphreys, Chief Topographical Engineer, by conducting reconnaissance missions and drew detailed maps of appropriate routes for the army in its advance up the peninsula. On May 18, 1862 he was given command of the 3rd Brigade, 2nd Division, V Corps, which he led at Gaines' Mill (where he was wounded but refused to be taken from the field), Malvern Hill, Harrison's Landing, Second Bull Run, Antietam and Fredericksburg. He was promoted to brigadier general on September 26, 1862. With the reorganization of the Army of the Potomac by General Hooker in February 1863, he was appointed chief topographical engineer and then chief engineer. Breveted a major general on May 3, 1863, he distinguished himself on the second day (July 2) at Gettysburg. Recognizing the importance of the undefended position on the left flank of the Union Army, he initiated its defense by directing, on his own initiative, the brigade of Colonel Strong Vincent to occupy Little Round Top just minutes before the Confederate attack. He next commanded the II Corps at Auburn, Bristoe Station, Kelly's Ford and Mine Run. In charge of the V Corps, Army of the Potomac, throughout most of the Petersburg campaign, he was relieved of command by Sheridan for not promptly committing it to action at Five Forks on April 1, 1865. He was finally exonerated by the Warren Court of Enquiry 14 years later in 1881. However, professionally ruined, he is said to have "died of a broken heart" nine months later.

A lieutenant of the 4th Infantry in the Northwest before the Civil War, **Philip "Little Phil" Sheridan** held a number of administrative posts before being given command of troops. He served as chief quartermaster and commissary of the Army of Southwest Missouri, under Major General Samuel Curtis, and was quartermaster at the headquarters of General Halleck when appointed colonel of the 2nd Michigan Cavalry on May 25, 1862. After only eight days he was given command of the 2nd Brigade, Cavalry Division, Army of the Mississippi, and was promoted to brigadier general one month later based on a hard-fought victory at Booneville, Mississippi. He was next given command of the 11th Division, Army of the Ohio, and distinguished himself at Perryville, Kentucky, on October 8, 1862, when he launched a successful counterattack after holding a well-organized position. At Stones

LEFT
Gouverneur Kemble Warren was born at Cold Spring. He entered West Point at age 16 and graduated second in a class of 44 cadets in 1850. Commissioned a brevet second lieutenant, he worked on transcontinental railroad surveys and helped map the trans-Mississippi West. He was a mathematics instructor at West Point when the Civil War began. (Library of Congress LC-B8172-1757)

RIGHT
Born in New York in 1831, Philip "Little Phil" Sheridan was suspended during his third year at West Point for fighting, and hence graduated a year late in 1853. He was only 5 foot 5 inches tall; Lincoln described him as having "a long body, short legs, not enough neck to hang him, and such long arms that if his ankles itch he can scratch them without stooping." (US National Archives NWDNS-111-B-2520)

River, Tennessee, on December 31, 1862, he earned his second star commanding the 3rd Division, Right Wing, XVI Corps, Army of the Cumberland. He then led the 3rd Division, XX Corps at Winchester, Tennessee, and the 2nd Division, IV Corps, at Chickamauga. He further distinguished himself during the Chattanooga Campaign when elements of his division broke through the Confederate lines on Missionary Ridge and came close to capturing Braxton Bragg and several of his generals. On April 4, 1864 Grant appointed him to command the Cavalry Corps, Army of the Potomac, following which he conducted his Richmond Raid between May 9 and 24, which resulted in the defeat and death of Confederate cavalry commander "Jeb" Stuart at Yellow Tavern. From August, 1864 through February 1865 he commanded the Army of the Shenandoah, plus the Middle Military Division, during which time he undertook his brilliant Valley Campaign, winning victories at Winchester, Fishers Hill and Cedar Creek. He was largely responsible for the decisive Union victory at Five Forks shortly after joining the Army of the Potomac outside Petersburg in late March 1865.

OPPOSING ARMIES

Nearly 160,000 soldiers, plus several thousand staff officers and support personnel, and tens of thousands of civilians, were involved in the Petersburg campaign, which began on June 9, 1864 and ended with the collapse of the Confederate lines on April 2, 1865. Robert E. Lee commanded the remnants of the Army of Northern Virginia, which by June 1864 amounted to only 54,751 men, consisting of 41,810 infantry, 5,520 artillery and 7,421 cavalry. Meanwhile, the much stronger Union army under Ulysses S. Grant was composed of 85,370 infantry, 8,005 artillery and 14,044 cavalry.

Lee's depleted forces consisted of the First, Second and Third corps, under generals James Longstreet, John B. Gordon and Ambrose P. Hill, respectively, plus the Fourth Corps commanded by Richard Heron Anderson and the Cavalry Corps under Wade Hampton.

Each of the first three Confederate army corps was made up of three infantry divisions commanded by a major general who was supported by a large group of staff officers including adjutants, quartermasters, commissaries and surgeons. Anderson's Fourth Corps possessed only two divisions. Hampton's cavalry corps also consisted of only two divisions, plus a brigade of horse artillery under Major R. Preston Chew. Each Confederate division consisted of four brigades of infantry each containing from four to seven regiments, plus artillery composed of five battalions comprising from three to five individual batteries.

The Confederate First Corps had returned from hard service in Tennessee to join Lee for the Wilderness campaign, only for its commander, James Longstreet, to be seriously wounded by friendly fire on May 6, 1864. Out of action until October 19, when he was placed in command of forces at Bermuda Hundred and north of the James River, his corps was under R.H. Anderson for much of the early part of the Petersburg campaign. The smallest in Lee's army, the Second Corps numbered only 8,600 effectives by the time it arrived in the Petersburg defenses under the temporary command of John B. Gordon in December 1864. This corps had been led by Jubal Early since May of that year, when Gordon received permanent command after Early's humiliating defeat at Waynesboro on March 2, 1865. Formed during the reorganization of Lee's army following Chancellorsville, A.P. Hill's Third Corps came into being on May 30, 1864, and fought in all the major battles of the Army of Northern Virginia until Hill's death on April 2, 1865. Following this, its troops were merged into the First Corps. The Fourth Corps was organized in late 1864 with R.H. Anderson in command following Longstreet's return to the First Corps in October of that year.

Under the ultimate command of U.S. Grant, the Army of the Potomac, led by George G. Meade, was composed of the II, V, VI and IX corps. Commanded by Major General Benjamin Butler, the Army of the James consisted of the X and XVIII Corps. Each of these corps was composed of three infantry divisions plus a brigade of artillery, with the exception of the IX Corps, which had a fourth division.

Photographed by Matthew Brady *c.* 1860, this view of Petersburg depicts a peaceful and industrious community with thriving trade and communications on the banks of the Appomattox River prior to the Civil War. (US National Archives NWDNS-111-B-84/ NWDNS-111-B-108)

Commanded by W.S. Hancock from the beginning of the Petersburg campaign until November 26, 1864, when Andrew A. Humphrey took over, the II Corps had "a record of longer continuous service, a larger organization, hardest fighting, and greatest number of casualties, than any other in the Eastern armies," according to historian Francis Trevelyn Miller. Its members were identified by a flannel cloth trefoil, or three-leaf clover, worn generally on their cap tops, after the general introduction of the corps badge system to the Army of the Potomac in the spring of 1863. Created on March 3, 1862 as part of McClellan's Army of the Potomac, the V Corps was under the command of G.K. Warren throughout the entire Petersburg campaign and was distinguished by a corps badge in the shape of a Maltese cross. Recognized by a cross of St Andrew corps badge, the VI Corps was under H.G. Wright, its former commander John Sedgwick having been killed at Spotsylvania on May 9, 1864. The IX Corps was described by historian William F. Fox as, "A wandering corps, whose dead lie buried in seven states." Originally formed from troops of the Department of the South and from Burnside's Expeditionary Corps for operations in North Carolina, it had served in the Department of the Ohio for a year before returning east in April 1864 to be placed once more under Burnside. As both he and his chief of staff John G. Parke were senior to Meade, the IX Corps was placed under the direct command of Grant, and not officially made part of the Army of the Potomac. Burnside was finally relieved of command on August 14, 1864 for an unsatisfactory performance during the Petersburg mine assault. Parke replaced him in command until the end of the war. The badge for this corps was a shield crossed by anchor and cannon.

Wearing the badge of the square bastion, the X Corps was transferred from the Department of the South in April 1864, while the XVIII Corps, bearing the trefoil cross, had been organized from troops in the Department of North Carolina in December 1862. Both became part of the Army of the James when it was organized under Butler in April 1864, and both were deactivated on December 3, 1864 to create the XXIV and XXV corps. The former was created from the white troops of the X and XVIII corps, and was commanded by E.O.C. Ord from December 3 to 6, 1864; Alfred H. Terry until January 2, 1865; Charles Devens, Jr to January 15; and John Gibbon to April 27, 1865. Established on the same date, the XXV Corps was composed of the black units previously belonging to the X and XVIII corps, and was commanded by Godfrey Weitzel from December 3, 1864 to January 1, 1865; C.A. Heckman to February 2; and Weitzel again until the end of the campaign. The corps badges of these two organizations were heart and diamond (or lozenge) shaped respectively.

OPPOSING PLANS

Located only 22 miles south of Richmond, and ten miles from the James River at City Point, Petersburg was a major supply centre and main artery for the Confederate capital. Known as "The Cockade City," it had a population of about 1,600 in 1861. On the Appomattox River, vessels of about 100 tons ascended to the Port of Petersburg and those of larger size to Waltham's Landing, six miles to the south. Extensive facilities for business in the city processed and transported cotton, tobacco and metal produced in the area. With the development of transport technology during the first half of the 19th century, Petersburg became established as a railroad centre. The Lynchburg & Petersburg Railroad provided an important link with Farmville and Lynchburg in western Virginia, while the Petersburg & Weldon Railroad enabled a valuable supply line with Weldon, North Carolina, to the south. The South Side Railroad from Petersburg was also a vital resource for the Confederacy, carrying food from southwest Georgia. The section of this line to the east of the city linked Petersburg with City Point, a small port town at the confluence of the James and Appomattox rivers. Until 1862, when most of it fell into Union hands, the Norfolk & Petersburg Railroad provided a vital link with the coast. Once supplies arrived in Petersburg they were transported via the Richmond & Petersburg Railroad to the Confederate capital.

Numerous plank roads converging on Petersburg likewise added to the strategic importance of the city. These were constructed using pine and oak planks, eight feet long, one foot wide and four inches thick, laid across parallel beams slanted toward a ditch. The first all-weather route connecting the tobacco and wheat farms of southern Virginia with the market – the Boydton Plank Road – extended 73 miles southwest to Clarksville, near the North Carolina border. The Jerusalem Plank Road also ran south out of the city toward Jerusalem, on the Nottoway River. Several roads, including a turnpike, ran from Petersburg to Richmond west of the James River. By 1864, both Lee and Grant knew that if these routes were cut, Petersburg would no longer be able to provide Richmond with much needed supplies and subsistence. Without his lifeline, Lee would be forced to evacuate both cities and the Confederacy would be doomed.

THE OPENING PHASE

THE "BATTLE OF OLD MEN AND YOUNG BOYS," JUNE 9, 1864

The siege of Petersburg may not have been necessary if an operation mounted by Major General Benjamin F. Butler, commanding elements of the Army of the James at Bermuda Hundred, had been successful. While the main armies of Grant and Lee were still recoiling from the results of battle at Cold Harbor, three cavalry regiments under Brigadier General Augustus V. Kautz, with three infantry brigades, plus six field-pieces, amounting to about 4,500 men, were ordered to attack Petersburg. At that time the city was defended by only a small force under the overall command of Brigadier General Henry A. Wise, which manned the defenses around the land and water approaches to the city. Known unofficially as the "Dimmock Line" for Captain Charles Dimmock, who had also supervised the construction of the Richmond defenses, the finished works around Petersburg were placed on high ground and had batteries and salients projecting in front of the main defenses so the defenders could deliver enfilade fire up and down the lines.

The Union attack as first devised on June 1, 1864 was to be commanded by Brigadier General Edward W. Hinks, but Quincy Gillmore requested and received permission to lead the operation, despite his unpopularity with Butler. It involved a rapid advance on Petersburg to cut the Weldon Railroad and, if possible, "dash into the place [and] burn the public buildings and bridges." The infantry, consisting of the 2nd Brigade, First Division, Army of the James, under Colonel Joseph R. Hawley, and 1st and 2nd brigades, Second Division, Army of the James, under Brigadier General Edwards W. Hinks, was to make "a demonstration" from the east of the city via the City Point and Jordan's Point roads. Meanwhile, the cavalry under Kautz, consisting of three regiments of the 1st Brigade, Cavalry Division, XVIII Corps, was to launch the real attack from the south along the Jerusalem Plank Road. Learning from a deserter on the night of June 7 that there was "but one regiment guarding the south side of Petersburg, aided by the militia," Butler saw an opportunity to capture Petersburg and ordered the action to begin the following night.

As planned, the infantry was to set out at midnight on June 8 in advance of the cavalry in order to reach their designated points of attack ahead of the mounted troops, but things went wrong from the outset. According to Captain Theodore Bacon, commanding the 7th Connecticut, the infantry column "moved slowly on account of the condition of the roads." Kautz

The "battle of old men and young boys," June 9, 1864

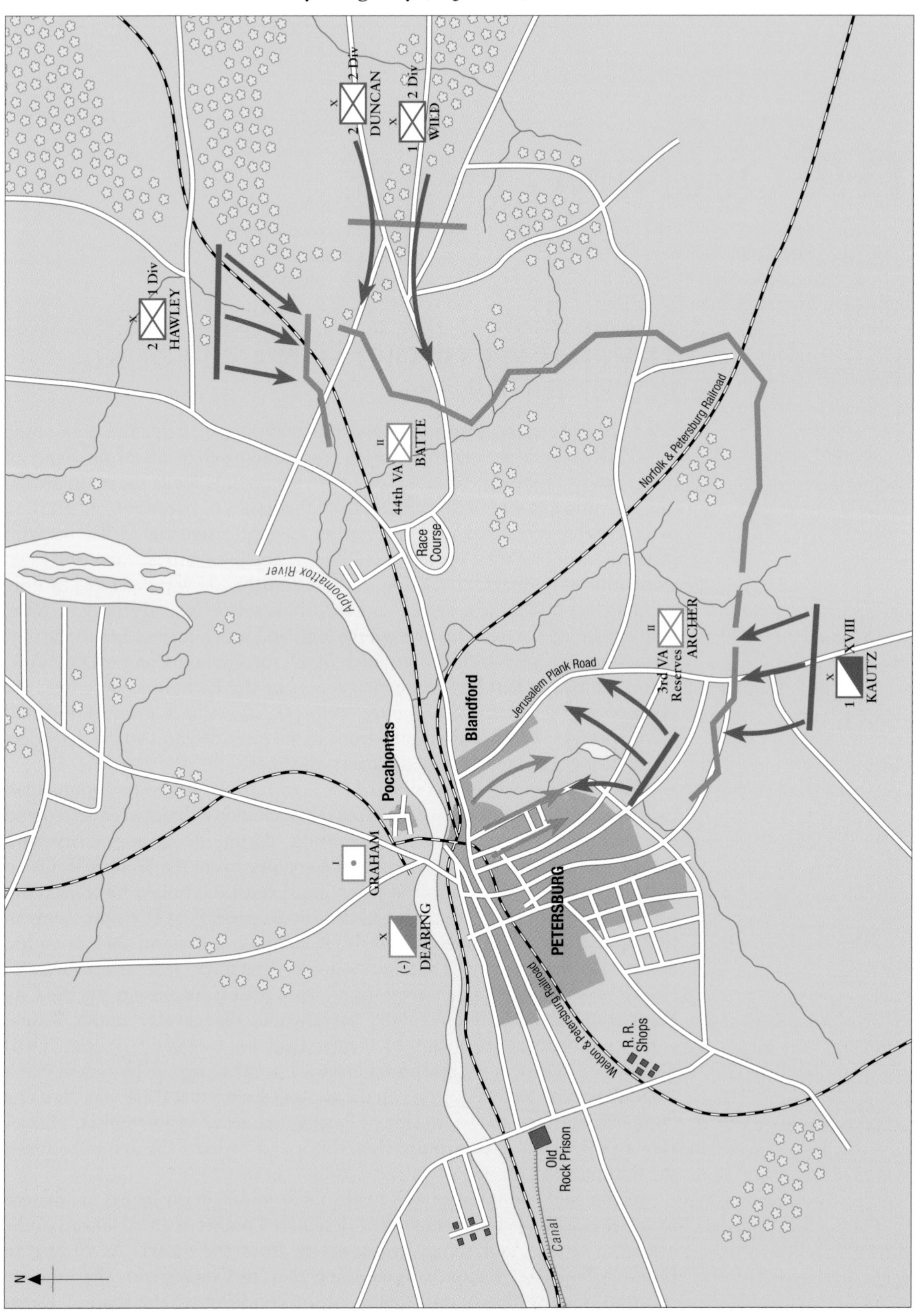

recorded in his diary that "the infantry lost its way in the woods," which delayed the whole force from getting across the pontoon bridge over the Appomattox River. As a result, the operation lost the element of surprise.

Taking a circuitous route to the east of Petersburg, the mounted units pressed on toward the "Southside" of the city, while the infantry under Gillmore and Hinks also began their approach. The Confederates were alerted to the presence of the enemy at about 1 a.m., which was followed by "three distinct discharges of cannon," and at about 7.30 a.m. the US Colored Troops under Hinks were driving in the Rebel pickets along the Jordan's Point Road, while the troops under Gillmore approached more cautiously along the City Point Road. By 8 a.m. a general alarm was sounded in Petersburg and, according to an account in the local press, "the Court house and engine bells were rung, to which the citizens responded with their usual alacrity, and manifested every disposition to defend their homes and firesides." The forces initially available to defend Petersburg consisted of a battalion of reserves, subsequently organized on June 15, 1864 as the 3rd Battalion, Virginia Reserves, commanded by Lieutenant Colonel Fletcher H. Archer, a Mexican War veteran; and the 44th Virginia Battalion under Major Peter V. Batte. Consisting of several hundred "old men and young boys," this greatly outnumbered force was required to hold back the much larger Union forces until reinforcements arrived.

Although armed with antiquated weapons, elements of the Petersburg Reserves manned the breastworks to the east of the city. Finding his black troops exposed to their flanking fire because the other Union infantry column had failed to advance along the City Point Road in support, Hinks received word from Gillmore that "the enemy was advancing in a strong line against his left," and that he was forced to withdraw. With little choice, Hinks also withdrew his brigade and the infantry assault had failed. In his report on return to camp, Gillmore inaccurately stated that Confederate reinforcements had arrived, and that he could not carry "the works in his front." A company commander of the 1st US Colored Troops blandly recorded, "Went to outworks of Petersburg. Skirmished and returned."

Meanwhile, Kautz's Union cavalry eventually reached the breastworks of the Dimmock Line across the Jerusalem Plank Road to the south of the city about midday on June 9. According to an account by a member of the Petersburg Reserves published in the local press, the Yankees maneuvered for a while and then ordered "a charge, and came down to our breastworks with a yell, their drawn sabres flashing in the sunlight. When within forty paces of the fortifications the order to fire was given, and the Yankees recoiled and fell back ... This charge was repeated twice, but with like results, when the enemy resorted to the flanking process, which, by reason of his overwhelming numbers, he was enabled to do with much ease. A short time afterwards a regiment came around Rives' house on our left, another appeared on our right, and a large body came down in front. We had but one hundred and seventy men all told, and it was impossible with this number to guard centre, right, and left, along a length of three quarters of a mile or more. The order was given to retreat, and in a few minutes the enemy had possession of our works ... and were in full pursuit of our men."

Couriers were dispatched for reinforcements, but they did not come up in time to save the fortifications, and many of Petersburg's "old men and young boys" in the ranks of the reserves, including William C. Bannister, "for many years an accountant in the Exchange Bank," George B. Jones, "a prominent

OPPOSITE PAGE
This map is based on that published in the *Official Military Atlas of the Civil War* between 1891 and 1895, which in turn was copied from an original document accompanying the report of General Benjamin Butler on his abortive attack on Petersburg on June 9, 1864. The original Petersburg defense works, known as the Dimmock Line, are in red.

druggist of Petersburg," and John Crowder, "a noble youth," were among the nine killed and 21 wounded.

The Confederate reinforcements that eventually arrived consisted of the Petersburg Artillery, also known as Graham's Battery, commanded by Captain Edward Graham, and elements of the cavalry brigade commanded by Brigadier General James Dearing, which consisted of the 8th Georgia, 4th North Carolina (59th Regiment NC Troops), and 12th and 16th North Carolina battalions. The account by a member of the local militia continued, "They were almost in Petersburg – could see its spires and steeples and many of the houses on our suburban limits – but ... the city was saved from the tread of the ruthless invader. Just at this opportune moment Graham's battery reached the Reservoir Hill, unlimbered in an instant [and] threw into the ranks of the enemy a shower of shell. The missiles of death coming so unexpectedly to the foe, he at first seemed overwhelmed with surprise, and halted, neither advancing nor retreating. But a minute or two later another branch of our service made its appearance, which quickly determined the enemy as to the best course for him to pursue. Dearing's cavalry brigade quickly dismounted, and descending the hill with a yell, charged upon the enemy in beautiful style. This was more than they expected, (since they had encountered but a few militia in the breastworks, and had advanced nearly a mile without seeing any regulars) and they instantly wheeled their horses and started back up the hill in great confusion. Graham's battery continued to play upon them, and Dearing's men crossed the ravine and ascended the opposite hill, in gallant style, their carbines keeping up a regular and most musical fusillade."

As they fell back, the Union cavalrymen brought off 42 prisoners and a 12-pounder gun captured by the 1st DC Cavalry. Due to the poor performance and lack of determination of General Gillmore, a valuable opportunity to capture Petersburg had been lost. On his return to camp, Butler demanded a full report explaining why the opportunity to break through the thinly manned Confederate defenses had been squandered. With the feud between Butler and Gillmore rumbling on, Grant transferred Gillmore to Washington, DC, where he successfully organized new recruits and invalids into a 20,000-man force to help protect the city from a threat by 10,000 Confederates under Jubal A. Early, who had reached the outer defenses of the Union capital on July 11–12, 1864. Wounded while pursuing Early's retreat, he recovered to command the Department of the South and the X Corps again until June 28, 1865.

CROSSING THE JAMES RIVER, JUNE 9–15, 1864

Despite Butler's abortive sortie toward Petersburg on June 9, 1864, Lee remained convinced that Grant's main army would operate north of the James River. As a result, he retained the bulk of his forces around Richmond. Meanwhile, two days after the disastrous assault at Cold Harbor Grant made the decision to cross the James River to cut the critical rail and road junctions south of Petersburg. To accomplish this he quietly withdrew 100,000 soldiers from a 10-mile front line, negotiated 50 miles of swampy ground and crossed a half-mile-wide tidal river. The 15th New York Engineers, under General Henry W. Benham, constructed the necessary pontoon sections behind the main Union lines at Cold Harbor on June 11. The same day, Grant ordered Major General George Gordon Meade to prepare the Army of the Potomac for movement on June 12. Major General Gouverneur K. Warren's V Corps were the first to pull out of the trenches near Richmond at 6 p.m. that day. The first obstacle en route to Petersburg was the Chickahominy River running in a southeasterly direction below the Union position at Cold Harbor. Arriving at Long Bridge before midnight, Warren's troops encountered Confederate pickets, which were driven back with a well-placed volley of musketry fire. The engineers immediately went to work clearing away the demolished bridge span and deployed their pontoon sections across the river. By midnight the cavalry was crossing the bridge, followed closely by the infantry. Once over the river, Warren's corps was assigned the task of feinting toward Richmond and covering the right flank of Grant's main movement.

At sunset on June 12, activity began along the entire length of the Union line at Cold Harbor. Major General William Farrar Smith's XVIII Corps departed due east for White House on the Pamunkey River, where they boarded river transports to join the Army of the James operating on the Bermuda Hundred peninsula near City Point, Virginia. Major General Winfield S. Hancock's II Corps and Major General H.G. Wright's VI Corps withdrew to the secondary line of trenches erected days earlier by the engineers. At 11 p.m. Hancock's corps departed to follow Warren's men across the Chickahominy at Long Bridge. They were followed by the VI Corps which struck out toward Jones Bridge about three miles downstream. Major General Ambrose Burnside's IX Corps departed from the right flank of the line and followed Wright's corps to Jones Bridge. Bringing up the rear of the Union withdrawal were cavalry troopers and a scattering of pickets left on the lines until almost daybreak on June 13. Soldiers' accounts of the march recall a bright moonlit night obscured by the choking dust of thousands of shuffling feet. According to J.T. Connolly, "This was a terrible forced march, lasting all one night, and next day, and half of the ensuing night, before we halted to eat or sleep."

South of the Chickahominy, Union engineers began the construction of 12 miles of defenses to protect the crossing point on the James River. By late afternoon, Hancock's men had arrived from the Long Bridge and occupied these positions. That evening Grant's headquarters removed to Wilcox's Landing on the James River. Meanwhile, engineers assisted by II Corps soldiers felled hundreds of trees to clear the path for the sections of pontoon bridge being brought up to lay across the James. This operation included the building of a 150-foot pier across a swamp on the north side. During the morning of June 14, the pontoons at Jones Bridge were removed as the last of the infantry crossed over the Chickahominy River. At Wilcox's Landing, the II Corps left their defensive positions and began crossing the James River by boat.

In the meantime, Grant's supply train bypassed the Chickahominy crossings at Long and Jones bridges and continued eastward to Cole's Landing. The pontoon bridge constructed there was the longest of the Chickahominy crossings, measuring 1,200 feet. The swampy terrain required extensive use of corduroy approaches to this bridge. The 1,200-foot span was completed after dark on June 14, and the supply train began moving across the bridge during the night. The longer route to the Cole's Landing crossing prevented the supply train from encumbering the movement of the main army, which was a constant concern for Grant and his quartermasters.

On the afternoon of June 14, 450 engineers began construction of the pontoon bridge across the James River. Work began simultaneously from Weyanoke Point on the north bank and near Windmill Point on the south.

The James River Pontoon Bridge was completed in only eight hours on June 8–9, 1864, by 450 engineers under Captain G.H. Mendell, who were initially directed by Major J.C. Duane and then by General Henry W. Benham. Working from both sides, 101 pontoons and three schooners were used to span the 2,100-foot width of the James River to enable the Army of the Potomac to cross the river in order to commence the assault on Petersburg. (Library of Congress LC-B8171-7484)

OPPOSITE PAGE
On June 12, 1864, the Army of the Potomac realized the worst fears of Robert E. Lee by crossing the James River. Within three days, Grant had moved five divisions within striking distance of Petersburg, with the main objective of cutting the supply routes converging on that city en route for Richmond, Virginia.

Constructed with 101 wooden pontoons, the bridge carried a roadbed 11 feet wide, and was lashed to six schooners anchored upstream to hold the bridge against the current. Three of these schooners held in place a 100-foot removable section that allowed gunboats and other vessels to pass through the bridge. Farther upstream, Butler had five stone-laden ships sunk in the channel to prevent Confederate gunboats from coming downstream to disrupt the operation. Taking nine hours to complete, the bridge was ready to receive traffic at 1 a.m. on June 15. When finished, the bridge was 2,100 feet in length, making it the longest floating bridge in military history.

Soon after its completion, troops and trains began crossing the bridge. The infantry of the IX Corps, a division of the VI Corps, and Wilson's Cavalry Division went via this route. However, most bridge traffic consisted of the large supply train arriving from Cole's Landing, plus cannon, limbers and caissons of the artillery, ambulances, baggage wagons and about 3,500 beef cattle. Among the personnel crossing the bridge on the first day were General Grant and his headquarters staff. Three hours after Union troops began crossing the James River pontoon bridge Hancock's II Corps completed its crossing of the James by boat. Delayed by difficulties in communications, this force arrived too late to assist the XVIII Corps in the initial assault on Petersburg on the evening of June 15.

After crossing the James River, the supply train was parked in and around the small hamlet of City Point and the City Point Railroad. A supply base had been established at this location during the weeks prior to the James River crossing by elements of Butler's Army of the James. An ideal location because of its position at the confluence of the James and Appomattox rivers, City Point allowed large seagoing vessels to dock at its waterfront. Separate

Crossing the James River, June 12–15, 1864

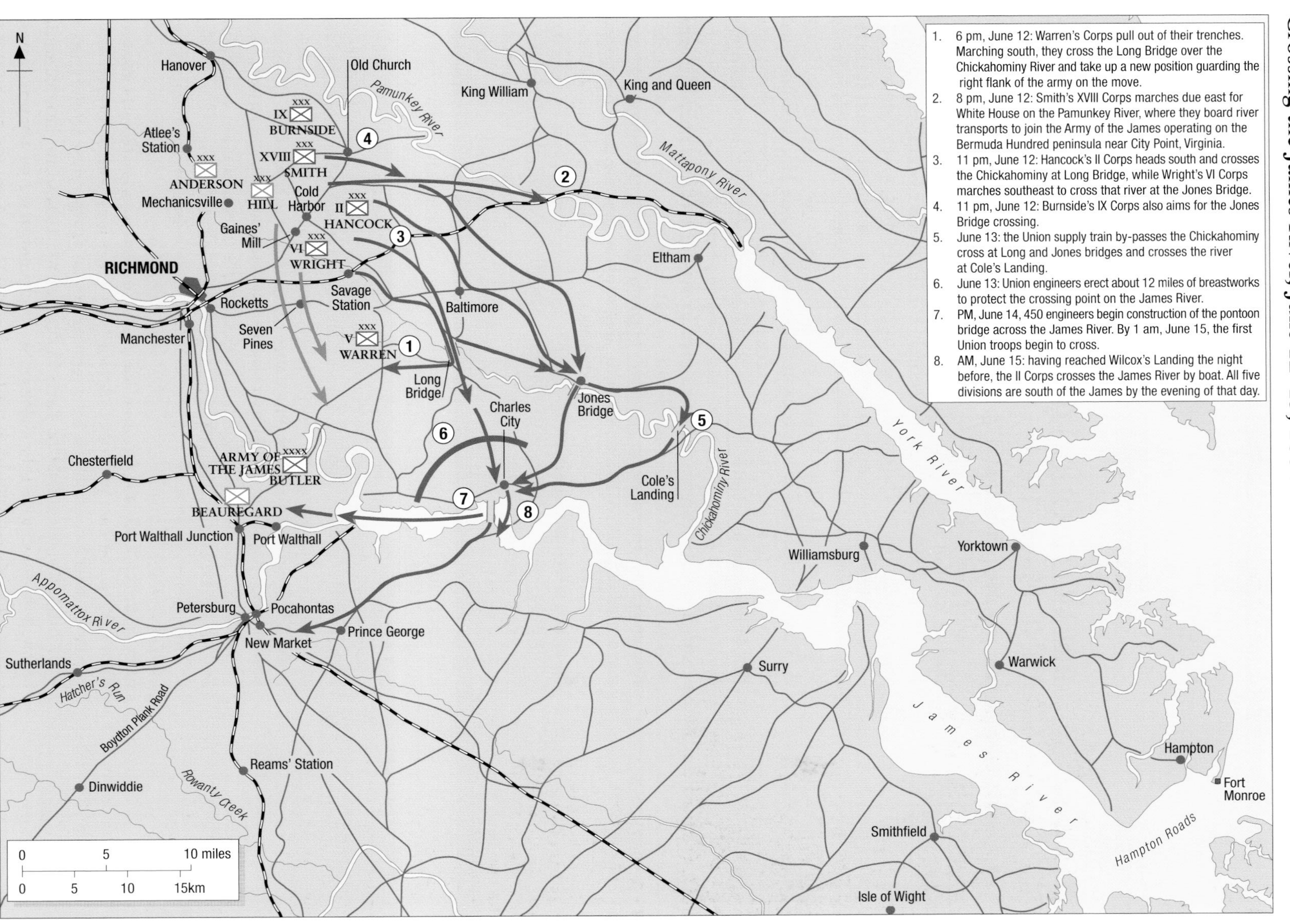

facilities were constructed to store commodities such as ammunition, clothing, subsistence, forage, medical supplies and camp equipment. On a daily basis, approximately 40 steamboats, 75 sailing ships and 100 barges operated from its wharves. By the fall of 1864, 20 miles of railroad constructed by the Railroad Construction Corps stretched from City Point to the rear of the Union siege lines, and about 18 trains daily made the trip to the front delivering supplies and evacuating casualties to the hospital complex at City Point.

BREAKTHROUGH ON THE DIMMOCK LINE, JUNE 15–18, 1864

Lee was completely fooled by Grant's move across the James River. For several days, the Confederate commander held the bulk of his army in their lines in front of Richmond. He did not move south across the James until June 18, and even then was not entirely convinced that Grant's entire army was across the river. Thus, when the Union XVIII Corps, under General W.F. "Baldy" Smith, arrived at the eastern approaches to Petersburg on June 15, Beauregard had only half of Dearing's cavalry brigade and a single infantry brigade under the former Virginia governor (now Brigadier General) Henry A. Wise. Confederate reinforcements from the Bermuda Hundred lines had been ordered to march rapidly for Petersburg, but could not reach the city before late evening. Until then, the 2,200 men under Wise, plus Dearing's cavalry, were all that Beauregard had at his disposal.

After being delayed by a skirmish at Baylor's Farm, Smith's Corps marched in sight of the Dimmock Line at approximately 11 a.m. on June 15. Remembering the debacle at Cold Harbor, the veteran Union general performed exhaustive reconnaissance. Determining that the eastern expanse of Confederate defenses was manned primarily by artillery, he finally ordered an attack which began about 6 p.m.

Because the Confederate works were actually held only by elements of Ferrebee's dismounted 4th North Carolina Cavalry, supported by Graham's Battery, the Union troops advanced entirely as a skirmish line with intervals of two paces between each man. Entering a ravine between what the Confederates had designated Batteries 7 and 8 on the Dimmock Line, which was a weak point in the otherwise formidable Rebel breastworks, Smith's men were able to capture from the rear Battery 5, one of the strongest of the Confederate positions, which was a V-shaped salient containing 16 guns. Commanding the 13th New Hampshire, Colonel Aaron F. Stevens reported, "Advanced our line at about 6.15 p.m., when my skirmish line, consisting of about 400, the center being held by my regiment, assaulted the enemy's advance rifle pits ... Being the first to break the line of enemy's works around Petersburg, [we] captured four 12-pounder Howitzer iron guns, a large quantity of ammunition and about 150 prisoners. Lost about forty men and officers."

Meanwhile, the rest of that sector of the Confederate line, manned by the 26th and 46th Virginia Infantry, of Wise's brigade, was rapidly disintegrating. Men from the 1st, 4th, 6th and 22nd US Colored Troops (USCT) moved south along the enemy works. Among the other positions captured was Battery 9, which contained a three-gun section of Sturdivant's artillery, on a slight hill at the junction of the Jordan's Point and George Court House roads, two important routes into Petersburg. Two companies of the 1st USCT cleared obstacles around this work, and turned the captured guns on the

Confederates, allowing their regiment to charge. After his regiment overran another battery, Major John McMurray, 6th USCT, recalled, "The ditch was now full of men, and we began to climb up the face of the parapet. A man would run his bayonet into the side of the parapet, and another would use it as a step-ladder to climb up. As we were thus ascending I was wondering why the Johnnies behind the parapet were so quiet. It was now getting quite dark, and I felt sure that as fast as a 'colored troop' would put his head above the level of the parapet it would be shot off, or he would be knocked back into the ditch; and I fully expected the Sixth U.S. Colored Troops, officers and all, to find their death in that ditch. But they didn't. Not a bit of it. We climbed into the fort or battery only to find it empty. The last Confederate was gone, save one, a fair haired boy of 17 or 18 years, dead."

During this assault, Lieutenant William H. Appleton, Company H, 4th USCT, won the Medal of Honor for being the "first man of the Eighteenth Corps to enter the enemy's works." In his congratulatory order to his troops following this action, General Smith stated, "To the colored troops comprising the division of Gen. Hinks, the General commanding would call attention of his command. With the veterans of the 18th Corps they have stormed the works of the enemy and carried them, taking guns and prisoners, and in the whole affair they have displayed all the qualities of good soldiers."

By 9 p.m. the Federals had taken Batteries 3 through 13 – in all, nearly two miles of the Confederate line. Despite the possibility of having a clear path into Petersburg, Smith declined a night advance. Perturbed by a rumor circulating that Rebel reinforcements were on the way, he was also incapacitated by recurring bouts of malaria contracted during antebellum service in Florida. At midnight on June 15 he telegraphed Butler stating, "It is impossible for me to go further to-night, but unless I misapprehend the topography, I hold the key to Petersburg." Despite his optimism, the ailing Union general permitted the Confederates to withdraw about a mile to the rear of the captured section of the Dimmock Line, where they threw up hasty entrenchments along Harrison's Creek. Having squandered another opportunity to capture a weakly defended Petersburg, the Union army would soon be involved in a protracted siege operation. On July 19, 1864 Smith was relieved from command of the XVIII Corps and he spent the remainder of the war on "special duty."

Meanwhile, the Union II Corps, temporarily commanded by David B. Birney as General Winfield Scott Hancock was suffering from wounds incurred at Gettysburg, arrived to reinforce the attacking Federal columns. Darkness ended the fighting on June 15, but the attacks were renewed the next day. As a result, the line southeast of Petersburg also gave way. In response, Beauregard stripped forces under General Robert Hoke from the Howlett Line at Bermuda Hundred to defend the city, and urgently requested that Lee send more divisions, which drained the precious reserves from the Richmond lines. Reinforcements arriving in the Petersburg trenches consisted of Bushrod Johnson's Division, Anderson's Corps, and by dusk of that second day Beauregard could muster about 14,000 to face the Federals.

The third day of battle was practically a repetition of the preceding day, with more of the southern section of the Dimmock Line collapsing under continued Federal pressure. However, at about 12.30 a.m., June 18, Beauregard ordered his forces to begin a withdrawal from the line along Harrison's Creek to new positions, under the supervision of Colonel D.B. Harris, of the Engineer Department. Throughout the hours before dawn, the Confederates engaged in

Nicknamed "Baldy" at West Point because his hair was thinner than normal for his age, William Farrar Smith was shocked by the bloodshed he witnessed at Cold Harbor, after his XVIII Corps had been detached from Butler's Army of the James to reinforce Meade. As a result, he was reluctant to press home his breakthrough on the Dimmock Line outside Petersburg on June 15, 1864. He was relieved from field command four days later and placed on "special service" for the remainder of the war. (Library of Congress LC-B813-2160)

The black troops of the 22nd Colored Regiment, Duncan's Brigade, charge the Dimmock Line on June 15, 1864. Based on a sketch by Edwin Forbes, this engraving was published in *Frank Leslie's Illustrated Newspaper* on July 9, 1864. (Author's collection)

the construction of a new defense line with good fields of fire about a mile closer to Petersburg. Unavoidably, these new works were so close to Petersburg that the enemy would be able to bombard the city. Colonel Alfred Roman, aide to Beauregard, later recalled that "without a moment's rest the digging of the trenches was begun, with such utensils as had been hastily collected at Petersburg, many of the men using their bayonets, their knives, and even their tin cans, to assist in the rapid execution of the work."

A general assault of Union forces was ordered at 4 a.m. that day, but it was quickly established that the eastern section of the Dimmock Line had been abandoned, except for some skirmishers who were gradually forced back. Advancing across the Norfolk & Petersburg Railroad, the Northern troops continued until they were brought face to face with the muzzles of the defenders' guns. Meanwhile, Confederate reinforcements continued to pour in to fill the new lines of defense, and Lee arrived at Petersburg to direct operations in person.

A major Union attack involving elements of four corps was launched on the new Confederate line at about 3 p.m. on June 18. During the course of several futile assaults, the 1st Maine Heavy Artillery, commanded by Colonel Daniel Chaplin and serving as infantry, suffered the most severe losses of any regiment in a single engagement of the entire war. About 4 p.m. this 900-strong unit emerged from the concealment of the Prince George Court House Road, only to be met by a heavy crossfire. Commanding the 3rd Division, II Corps, General Gershom Mott recalled that the 1st Maine advanced from a fringe of pines, their well-dressed ranks surging on like "a blue wave crested with a glistening foam of steel." Lieutenant Horace H. Shaw, Company F, remembered, "The field became a burning, seething, crashing, hissing hell." In less than half an hour, the 1st Maine withdrew having sustained 241 dead and dying and 371 wounded.

Once again, fighting ended with the coming of darkness. The Federal attempt to capture Petersburg had failed, with a loss of about 10,000 men, compared with an estimated 4,000 Confederate casualties. The lines of battle before Petersburg were clearly drawn, and both armies now settled down for a long siege. On July 19, 1864, Grant telegraphed General Henry Halleck to "Please order Colonel Abbot's siege train forward." That simple command began nine months of the most sustained fighting and extensive building of fortifications seen thus far in the Civil War.

JERUSALEM PLANK ROAD (FIRST WELDON RAILROAD), JUNE 21–24, 1864

While the Union siege operations around Petersburg were being consolidated, Grant began a series of battles aimed at extending his siege lines to the west and cutting the rail link supplying Petersburg. On June 21 the II Corps, temporarily commanded by David B. Birney as Hancock was incapacitated by wounds incurred at Gettysburg, supported by the VI Corps, attempted to cut the Weldon Railroad south of Petersburg. This movement was preceded by the cavalry divisions of generals James H. Wilson and Augustus Kautz, consisting of 5,500 cavalry and 12 guns, which began tearing up the track on the railroad as the II Corps moved across the Jerusalem Plank Road. According to a report in the Petersburg *Express*, the troopers "cut the telegraph wires, burnt the water tanks, wood sheds, and office, and tore up

Based on a sketch by E.F. Mullen and published in *Frank Leslie's Illustrated Newspaper* on July 9, 1864, this engraving depicts African-American troops of Hink's division bringing in the guns of Sturdivant's battery, captured on June 15, 1864. White soldiers cheer them on in the background. (Author's collection)

A topographical engineer and staff officer, James H. Wilson was without previous cavalry experience when selected to head the newly established Cavalry Bureau in Washington in February 1864. Taking command of the 3rd Division, Cavalry Corps, Army of the Potomac, the following April, he led his troops during the Overland Campaign and in the Shenandoah Valley before involvement in operations south of Petersburg, which included the Wilson and Kautz Raid. (Library of Congress LC-B813-2074)

about 150 yards of the railroad track." Meanwhile, the two Union corps advanced across the Jerusalem Plank Road and through dense woods toward the railroad and built breastworks in which they lay that night, with the II Corps on the right and the VI Corps to its left.

As they continued their advance in line of battle at about noon the next day, Lee retaliated by ordering Wilcox's and Mahone's divisions of Hill's Third Corps, led by Brigadier General William Mahone, into the vicinity of Globe Tavern. A railroad engineer prior to the war, Mahone had worked on that stretch of track and had precise knowledge of the terrain. Hence, his division led the action. At 3 p.m., Mahone's division counterattacked through a gap created between Barlow's First Division, which formed the left wing of the Union II Corps, and Wright's VI Corps. This caused the unsteady Union infantry, who were busy once again entrenching, to panic and start fleeing back to the rifle pits erected the previous night. As Mahone's infantry charged north in line of battle behind the Union front line, they rolled back the rest of the II Corps consisting of Mott's Third Division, which also retreated in disorder to the breastworks. The right wing of the Confederates then crashed into the left wing of Gibbon's Second Division, capturing the guns of McKnight's battery.

The entire Union force thus fell back either into their previously occupied breastworks or beyond toward the Plank Road. Later that day a counterattack by elements of Gibbon's 2nd Division retook the breastworks to their front, forcing Hill's troops to withdraw to the line of the railroad. What remained of the II Corps lay on their arms in their re-captured breastworks that night.

On June 23, Wheaton's VI Corps continued the Union advance towards the railroad. Within two miles of their objective, they halted and entrenched with Grant's Vermont Brigade at the farthest point westward. Sharpshooters were sent forward to secure the railroad, and working parties actually reached it and began tearing up the rails, while other elements of the brigade were posted in scattered and isolated positions to provide protection from any Confederate interference.

Lee counterattacked again with Hill's Corps and Mahone's division swept over the railroad throwing the Vermonters into complete disarray, forcing them back to an entrenched position in the woods. Mahone next sent the brigade of Mississippians commanded by Nathaniel H. Harris around the north flank of the Vermonters while he ordered the remainder of his division south in an attempt to get around Wheaton's left flank. Weisiger's brigade of Virginians struck the 4th Vermont picket line splitting the regiment in half and fanned out in its rear.

Captain William C. Tracy assembled the left wing of the 4th Vermont and rallied his men for a brief stand. He soon fell dead, shot through the neck, and after several more men were killed or wounded the rest surrendered. Major Pratt and the right wing of the regiment fled north to join Major Fleming's battalion at his breastwork in the woods. The Florida Brigade advanced north and met the Mississippi Brigade moving south behind Fleming's breastwork. Escape was impossible and at dusk when their ammunition ran out, Majors Pratt and Fleming surrendered their commands totaling 344 officers and enlisted men.

Although Union forces were twice driven back from their advanced positions and had about 1,700 taken prisoner in total, they had destroyed some of the Weldon Railroad. They had also managed to extend their lines a few miles farther to the west, a strategy that Grant would employ throughout the remainder of the campaign.

THE WILSON AND KAUTZ CAVALRY RAID, JUNE 21–29, 1864

A German immigrant to the US, Augustus Valentine Kautz was a Mexican War veteran and Indian fighter before becoming an aggressive and competent Civil War cavalry leader. He received command of a cavalry division in the Army of the James on May 7, 1864 whilst receiving promotion to brigadier general of volunteers. In his memoir of involvement in the cavalry raid of June 25–29, 1864, he commented, "The successful destruction of the Danville [Rail]road was quite equalled by our retreat after being almost completely surrounded." (Library of Congress LC-BH82- 625)

After destroying further railroad south and southwest of Petersburg, General Wilson was under orders to make his way either to the coast or to General Sherman in North Georgia. If he could not cross the Roanoke River he was to decide which route to pursue in returning to the Army of the Potomac.

Hence, while Wilson's cavalry went to work on the Weldon Railroad, Kautz rode farther west via Dinwiddie Court House and cut the Southside Railroad between Sutherland and Ford's Station on the evening of June 22, destroying tracks, railroad buildings and two supply trains. Followed by Wilson, who was being pursued by Confederate cavalry, Kautz's command proceeded farther west during the early hours of the next day to the junction of the Richmond & Danville Railroad at Burke's Station, where they drove back more Confederate cavalry of General W.H.F. "Rooney" Lee's division.

Wilson followed Kautz along the Danville Railroad, destroying about 30 miles of track as he advanced. On June 24, while Kautz remained skirmishing around Burkeville, Wilson moved on to Meherrin Station on the Richmond & Danville Railroad and began destroying further track. On June 25 both Wilson and Kautz continued to destroy the track southwest toward the Staunton River Bridge, but were halted by a mixed body of 938 Confederate reserves commanded by Captain Benjamin L. Farinholt, 53rd Virginia Infantry, who killed and wounded about 250 Union troopers and prevented the destruction of the bridge. During this attack, Private Nelson W. Ward, Company M, 11th Pennsylvania Cavalry, earned the Medal of Honor for voluntarily taking part in a charge and going ahead alone to secure the body of his company commander, Captain Gerard Reynolds. Meanwhile, "Rooney" Lee's cavalry division closed on the raiders from the north, forcing them to abandon their attempts to capture and destroy the bridge. By this time, the Union cavalrymen were about 100 miles from their own lines, and many were suffering from hunger and sunstroke in the extremely hot weather.

Believing he had achieved much of his objective, Wilson ordered his division eastward the next day via Wylliesburg and Christianville, while Kautz's troopers withdrew after as a rearguard. Encountering further resistance as they crossed the Meherrin River on June 27, the Union column turned toward the Boydton Plank Road which it began to reach by nightfall. According to a journal entry of that date made by Augustus Kautz, "Quite a rain shower fell about dark and it was difficult to get to sleep. The rain was very refreshing and cooling. We have had extremely hot weather for several days. Men and horses are very much jaded. A large flock of Negroes have joined the column; that encumbers it very much. Our sick and wounded impede our progress."

Instead of marching up the plank road on June 28, the exhausted Union cavalry troopers again turned east and crossed the Nottoway River at Wyatt's Mill, but their progress was checked by elements of Wade Hampton's cavalry division at Stony Creek. Directed to take an alternative route via the Stage Road on June 29, Kautz met little resistance until near Ream's Station, where he was confronted by Forney's Brigade of Mahone's Division. According to his journal, "An Alabama regiment charged on our advance and about forty prisoners were captured and the regiment repulsed with heavy loss in the Eleventh Pennsylvania Cavalry in officers." Realizing he faced superior

Note: Gridlines are shown at intervals of 500yds/457m
CONFEDERATE FORCES
A Hill's 3rd Army Corps HQ
B Heth's Division
C Cooke's Brigade
D MacRae's Brigade
E Archer's Brigade
F Johnson's Brigade
G Wilcox's Division
H Thomas' Brigade
I Lane's Brigade
J McGowan's Brigade
K Scale's Brigade
L Mahone's Division
M Forney's Brigade
N Weisiger's Brigade
O Harris' Brigade
P Wright's Brigade
Q Finegan's Brigade
Walker's Artillery
XXX
III
HILL
WELDON AND
PETERSBURG RAILROAD

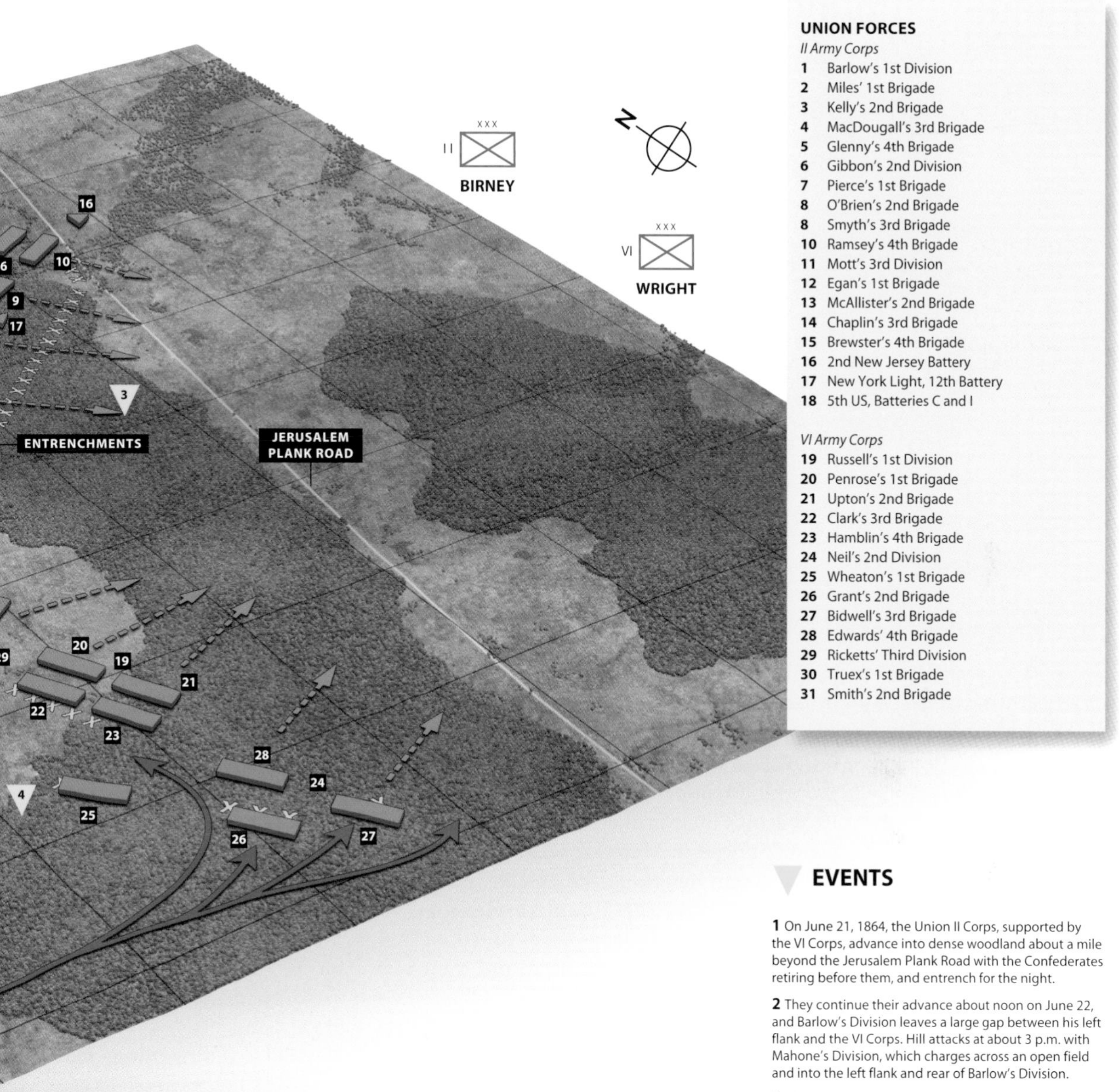

EVENTS

1 On June 21, 1864, the Union II Corps, supported by the VI Corps, advance into dense woodland about a mile beyond the Jerusalem Plank Road with the Confederates retiring before them, and entrench for the night.

2 They continue their advance about noon on June 22, and Barlow's Division leaves a large gap between his left flank and the VI Corps. Hill attacks at about 3 p.m. with Mahone's Division, which charges across an open field and into the left flank and rear of Barlow's Division.

3 Also hit in their front by the rest of Hill's Corps, most of the II Corps retreat in panic back to their entrenchments of the previous night, or to the plank road, leaving behind many dead, wounded or captured.

4 On June 23, Wheaton's VI Corps continues to advance towards the Weldon and Petersburg Railroad. Within two miles of their objective, they halt and entrench themselves with Grant's Vermont Brigade at the farthest point westward. Some advanced elements reach the railroad and begin tearing up the tracks.

5 Hill responds with Mahone's Division, which launches flanking attacks. This forces the VI Corps back towards the Jerusalem Plank Road, and much of the Vermont Brigade is captured.

BATTLE OF JERUSALEM PLANK ROAD (GURLEY FARM), JUNE 21–23, 1864

Grant's first attempt to extend his siege lines around the south side of Petersburg fails as Ambrose P. Hill's III Corps launches two decisive counterattacks using the veteran division of William "Little Billy" Mahone.

The cavalry under General James Wilson systematically destroy the Weldon Railroad during the cavalry raid of June 1864. Some of the accompanying artillery hold off a Confederate counterattack on the distant ridge, and horse-handlers mind the mounts, while the troopers destroy the track. General Wilson is seated in the foreground conferring with a scout or aide. (Author's collection)

numbers, Kautz decided entrenchment was his only course of action and breastworks were hastily thrown up using fence rails and felled trees. The fighting lasted from early in the morning until about 2 p.m. Holding his ground until Wilson's column began to arrive, it soon became evident that the Union troopers were surrounded. Before they could withdraw, a portion of Wilson's lines broke in confusion and ploughed back through elements of Kautz's division. Many of Wilson's remaining men were cut off, while Kautz succeeded in marching the greater part of his exhausted troops through the woods, crossing the Roanoke Railroad north of Rowanty Bridge, and reaching the main Union lines at about 9 p.m. that day. The remnants of Wilson's division eventually found their way back by crossing Blackwater Creek and following a circuitous route via the plank road from Suffolk to Prince George Court House.

Although the Union force sustained 1,500 killed, wounded or missing, and had to abandon most of its artillery, wagons and prisoners, few more effective operations of this kind were accomplished by cavalry during the Civil War. Marching nearly 500 miles in nine days, the troopers under Wilson and Kautz destroyed several stations and about 30 miles of track and other property on the Roanoke Railroad, plus a similar amount of track on the Danville Road. As a result, supply to the Confederate capital, and to the Army of Northern Virginia, was severely disrupted.

FIRST DEEP BOTTOM, JULY 27–29, 1864

On June 19, only a day after the failure of initial attempts to carry Petersburg by storm had failed, Grant ordered Butler to send a brigade to "seize, hold, and fortify the most commanding and defensible ground that can be found" back on the north side of the James River. This would create a bridgehead that could be defended, perhaps with the aid of gunboats in the James River,

Published in *Harper's Weekly* on August 6, 1864, this engraving depicts the return of Kautz's cavalry after the Union raid which destroyed much of the railroad south of Petersburg. The accompanying caption stated: "Both men and horses returned in a state of great exhaustion; the troops were without coats – blankets had been left behind – and in many cases even hats and caps were absent, their places being supplied by turbans, female head-gear, or whatever came to hand. Some had lost their horses, and rode mules; others, still worse off, had to lead their tired beasts. And thus ragged and weary, and presenting the most grotesque appearance, the column straggled in from the great raid." (Author's collection)

and from which future operations might be launched against Richmond. It was also hoped that the threat to the capital would force Lee to recall troops north of the James, thereby weakening the Petersburg defenses. The task was carried out on the night of June 20 by Brigadier General Robert S. Foster, commanding the Third Division, X Corps. Foster's force crossed over on a pontoon bridge and occupied the west side of Bailey's Creek, which flowed south into the James River at Deep Bottom. The mouth of the creek and the hydrology of the loop at that point on the James had created a deep-water area well suited for loading and unloading large vessels, and which had given the area the name Deep Bottom.

On July 23 Foster received further reinforcements, which strengthened the Union foothold. This caused Lee to react, ordering Kershaw's division from its position at Petersburg to the north side of the James via Chaffin's Bluff, in order to drive off the threatening Union force. Kershaw launched his attack on the morning of July 25 driving back the newly arrived Northern troops east of Bailey's Creek. As Union counterattacks were unable to retake the position, Grant ordered further reinforcements sent on July 27 which consisted of Hancock's II Corps, supplemented by two divisions of cavalry under Sheridan, plus Kautz's division of cavalry from the Army of the James. The main purpose of this action was to enable the Union cavalry to destroy the Virginia Central Railroad, the only rail link between Lee and the forces of Jubal Early that had recently raided north to Washington, DC. Another purpose was the continued diversion of Confederate troops from the Petersburg defenses north to Richmond. This would provide a greater chance of success for the planned attack on Petersburg by forces under Burnside in conjunction with a mine due to be exploded under the Confederate lines on July 30, 1864.

The Confederates constructing and manning the outer line of entrenchments facing Hancock near Bailey's Creek consisted of Kershaw's troops, amounting to only about 4,200 infantry; Hardaway's and Cutshaw's battalions of artillery;

The Wilson and Kautz cavalry raid, June 21–29, 1864

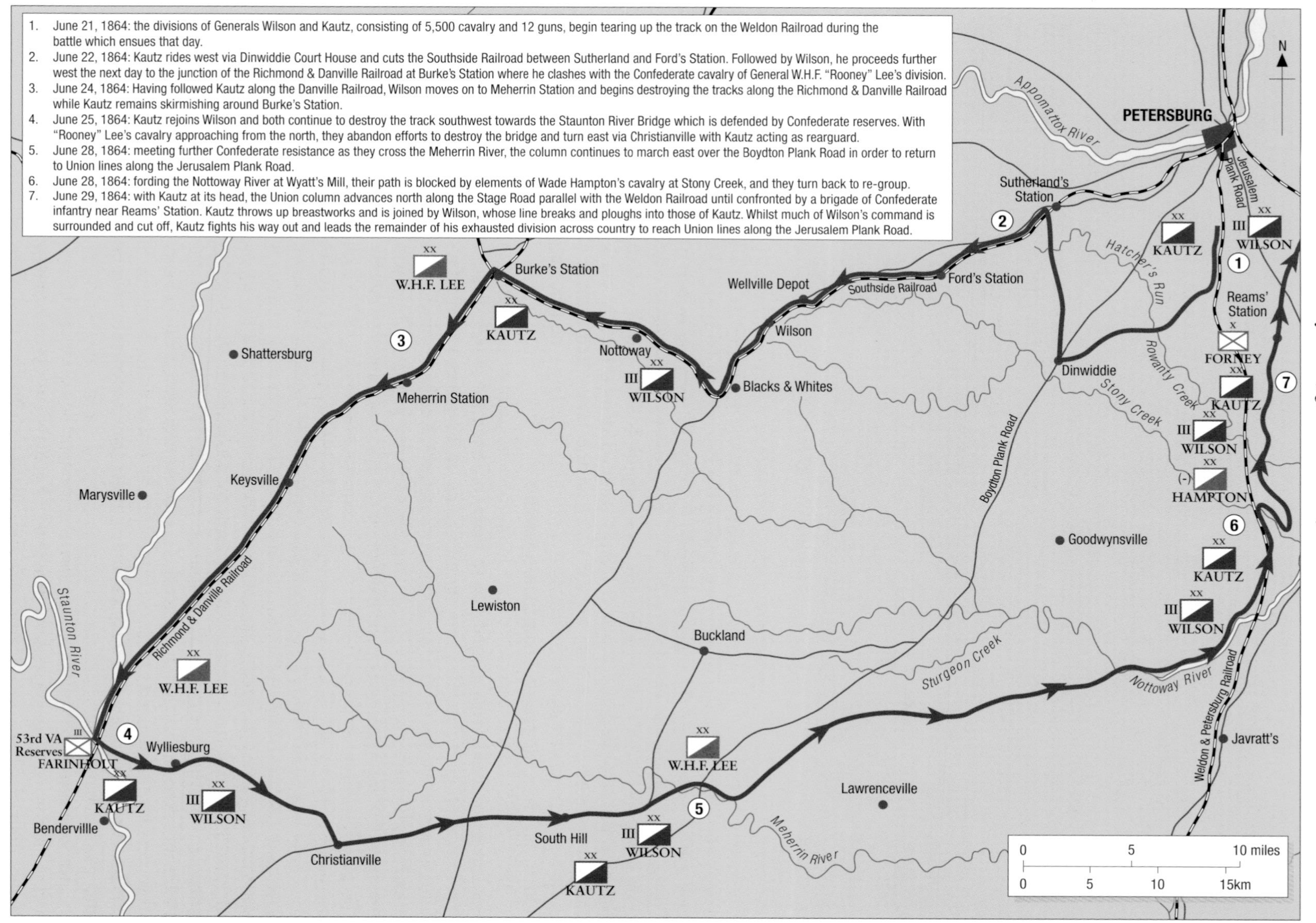

OPPOSITE PAGE Planning for what became known as the Wilson and Kautz raid began on June 20, 1864, two days after the failure of the attempt to take Petersburg by direct assault. Designed to destroy the railroads south of Petersburg, and involving about 5,500 Union cavalry plus 12 field guns, the operation was under overall command of Brigadier General James H. Wilson, whose cavalry division would be supported by that of Brigadier General Augustus V. Kautz. Marching nearly 500 miles in nine days, the Union troopers destroyed almost 80 miles of Confederate railroad, and severely disrupted the supply lines to Petersburg and Richmond, at a cost of over a quarter of their number.

UNION FORCES
Third Division (Army of the Potomac)
Brigadier General James H. Wilson

First Brigade
Colonel John B. McIntosh
1st Connecticut
3rd New Jersey
2nd New York
5th New York
2nd Ohio

Second Brigade
Colonel George H. Chapman
3rd Indiana
1st New Hampshire
8th New York
22nd New York
1st Vermont

Cavalry Division (Army of the James)
Brigadier General Augustus V. Kautz

First Brigade
Colonel Simon H. Mix
3rd New York
5th Pennsylvania

Second Brigade
Colonel Samuel P. Spear
1st District of Columbia
11th Pennsylvania

Third Brigade
Colonel Andrew W. Evans
1st Maryland
1st New York Mounted Rifles

CONFEDERATE FORCES
Cavalry
Lee's Division
Major General W. H. F. Lee.

Barringer's Brigade
Brigadier General Rufus Barringer
1st North Carolina
2nd North Carolina
3rd North Carolina
5th North Carolina

Beale's Brigade
Brigadier General R. L. T. Beale
9th Virginia
10th Virginia
13th Virginia

Dearing's Brigade
Brigadier General James Dearing
8th Georgia
4th North Carolina
12th North Carolina Battalion
16th North Carolina Battalion

Infantry
Mahone's Division
Brigadier General William Mahone

Forney's Brigade
Brigadier General William H. Forney
8th Alabama
9th Alabama
10th Alabama
11th Alabama
13th Alabama
14th Alabama

Reserves
Captain Benjamin L. Farinholt,
53rd Virginia Infantry

a small mounted force of about 600 men from General G.W.C. Lee's Richmond defenses, under Brigadier General Martin Gary; plus two brigades from Wilcox's division which held the lines at Chaffin's Bluff.

The initial Union advance along the New Market Road was successful, with elements of Mile's brigade, Barlow's division, capturing four 20-pounder Parrotts manned by the Rockbridge Artillery plus a number of prisoners. However, Hancock did not follow up this success quickly, or in force, with the result that the disorganized Confederates had the opportunity to form a defense line along Bailey's Creek. After weakly probing toward the hastily constructed Rebel breastworks for most of the morning, Hancock declined to storm them, but instead sent the cavalry division commanded by Major General Alfred T.A. Torbert probing northward along the creek. The Union troopers found that the Confederate position extended farther to their right than expected, which they believed blocked any advance by the cavalry. With about 24,000 men at his disposal, Hancock's reluctance to attack an inferior force may have been due to the fact that he was still affected by Mahone's devastating flank attack on his corps at Jerusalem Plank Road during the previous month. More probably, he was fooled by Kershaw's astute deployment of available Confederate troops along the hastily constructed breastworks. According to the report of Colonel James P. Simms, commanding a brigade of Kershaw's division, "The enemy advanced, but the major-general disposed of the troops in such a manner as to extend the line to such an extent as to make them believe that we had so great a force as to deter him from an attack; and thus he delayed the enemy until reinforcements came to our aid." As a result, an opportunity to cause a breakthrough that

ABOVE LEFT
A landing point at Deep Bottom on the north shore of the James River. Grant ordered elements of the Army of the James, commanded by General Benjamin Butler, to establish a bridgehead in the Deep Bottom area for future operations against Richmond, and to serve as a diversionary action against the Petersburg campaign. (US National Archives NWDNS-111-B-18)

ABOVE RIGHT
The capture of four 20-pound Parrott guns manned by the Confederate Rockbridge Artillery by Miles' Brigade, Barlow's Division, during the battle of First Deep Bottom on July 27, 1864, is depicted in this engraving published in *Harper's Weekly* on August 20, 1864. (Author's collection)

might have led to the capture the Confederate capital was lost once more, as Confederate reinforcements hurriedly arrived to bolster the lines.

Lieutenant General Richard H. Anderson reached Chaffin's Farm during the evening of July 27 and took command of Heth's and Kershaw's divisions. While a sufficient force was left under Heth to man the breastworks, Kershaw led four small infantry brigades in an indecisive attack on the Union right flank during the early hours of the next morning. Meanwhile, Grant ordered an envelopment of the Confederate left flank in order to free the cavalry for its raid on the Virginia Central Railroad. The result was confused fighting around New Market Heights and Fussel's Mill in which the Confederate infantry clashed with two Federal cavalry divisions. Although the Confederates captured a Federal artillery piece, they made little further progress. Learning that more reinforcements, including Field's division, Longstreet's Corps and W.H.F. Lee's cavalry division, were on their way, Kershaw ordered his infantry back to their lines after "a sharp engagement ... without any decided results."

With the knowledge that heavy Confederate reinforcements had arrived north of the James, Hancock ceased all thought of further offensive action. At 5 p.m. on July 29, 1864 Grant and Meade paid him a visit and determined to end active operations on that part of the front. Hancock would stay in place to hold the Confederates at Deep Bottom. At a cost of about 330 Union troops, the operations of Hancock and Sheridan had drawn sufficient numbers of Lee's infantry away from the Petersburg defenses. But could Grant take advantage of this temporary weakness in the Petersburg defenses? It was time to use the mine.

THE BATTLE OF THE CRATER

Gaining a reputation for independent command after his successful expedition against coastal installations in North Carolina, General Ambrose Burnside twice rejected an offer to command the Army of the Potomac before finally accepting the post on November 7, 1862, after further success at Antietam. Relieved of command following failure at Fredericksburg, he remained in the army in a subordinate position and by 1864 commanded the IX Corps, Army of the Potomac. His support for the abortive mine operation of July 30 of that year led to his final resignation on April 15, 1865. (Library of Congress LOT 9934, p. 13)

THE MINE

According to the report of General Ambrose Burnside, commanding the IX Army Corps, the plan to mine the Petersburg defenses began when several noncommissioned officers and privates of the 48th Pennsylvania, a regiment which contained a number of miners from Schuylkill County, in east-central Pennsylvania, suggested the idea to their commanding officer, Lieutenant Colonel Henry Pleasants, who was described as "a skillful and experienced mining engineer." Born in Buenos Aires, Argentina, in 1833, Pleasants lived in Pottsville, Schuylkill County, Pennsylvania, before the war, and helped cut the railroad tunnels through the Allegheny Mountains. An ancient tactic in siege warfare with a first recorded use by the Assyrian army in 850 BC, military mining was by no means a new idea and had been employed previously in the Civil War with only limited success on June 25, 1863 during the siege of Vicksburg. Despite this, Pleasants became convinced that a mine would result in a Union breakthrough at Petersburg.

In preparation for presenting the plan to his divisional commander, Brigadier General Robert B. Potter, Pleasants personally conducted a reconnaissance to determine where his mine should be laid, during which a divisional staff officer who accompanied him was wounded in the face. An ideal target in the Confederate defenses known as Elliott's Salient, was identified within a distance of only 130 yards from the works occupied by the IX Corps midway along the Union siege lines. Pleasants next discussed his plan with other engineers, and also requested a list of all those with mining experience in his regiment. By June 24, he had a plan of action to present to General Potter.

Two days later, Burnside received a letter from Potter stating that he believed "a mine could be run under the enemy's works ... by which a breach could be made, if it was thought advisable." After consultation between these two officers, Burnside authorized the commencement of mining and informed General Meade who later reported, "When the subject was brought to my knowledge I authorized the continuance of the operations, sanctioned them, and trusted that the work would at some time result in an important part in our operations." However, he had reservations about the choice of location for the mine, believing it was too exposed to flanking fire. Grant did not specifically approve of the operation, but rather "consented to its advancement."

The mine was commenced along the slope leading to Taylor's Creek, about 100 yards behind the trenches of the 48th Pennsylvania, at midnight on

June 25, 1864. The work was overseen by Sergeant Henry Reese, a red-headed Welshman from Minersville, Pennsylvania, and an experienced miner. At first, only a few men were involved, but as tunneling progressed, more men were required to assist with the labor. By July, all 400 officers and men of the 48th Pennsylvania were working on the operation, with men digging day and night in two-and-a-half-hour shifts. Their reward at the end of each shift was a draught of whiskey.

Pleasants and his men had to deal with both mundane and highly technical difficulties during the excavation. The initial problem faced was a lack of the necessary tools and materials. They lacked proper picks, wheelbarrows, planks and nails. Worse, there was no effort by those in higher command to provide them. But the Pennsylvania miners remained undaunted and improvised. According to Pleasants' after-action report, dated August 2, 1864, "The mining picks were made out of those used by our pioneers." Hand-barrows to carry away the soil were constructed using hickory sticks nailed to cracker boxes. In the regimental history, Pleasants stated, "I had to do all the work move all the earth in old cracker-boxes; I got pieces of hickory and nailed on the boxes in which we received our crackers, and then iron-clad them with hoops of iron taken from old pork and beef barrels." Lumber to provide support beams in the tunnel was acquired by tearing down an old bridge. They also scoured the camps of the IX Corps for wood and commandeered local sawmills. One of the most important items required was a theodolite, or surveying instrument, needed to plot the course of the mining. An accurate estimate of the location of the tunnel was essential if the operation was to succeed. However, Meade's engineering staff was skeptical of the success of the operation, and stubbornly refused to comply, so Burnside ordered the purchase of one in Washington, DC. The instrument finally received by Pleasants was old-fashioned, but served its purpose.

Next there was the problem of what to do with the soil removed on an hourly basis by the miners. It first had to be carried from the mine face to the tunnel entrance. As the Confederates were watching and had signal towers peering down into the Union lines, the soil had to be surreptitiously disposed of. If the defending troops noticed soil being carried away, they would detect the location of the mine, and hinder or destroy it with countermining. Thus, the soil was transported to the rear in cracker boxes, where it was concealed in undergrowth or cut bushes.

Providing ventilation for the teams working in the mine presented one of the most technical challenges. This problem had deterred other engineers in the Army of the Potomac from undertaking the mining project. Most other engineers also thought the projected distance of the tunnel was too great. But Pleasants and his miners turned soldiers produced an ingenious solution, based on the experience of some of them in the Welsh coal mines. According to their regimental historian: "The ventilation was accomplished in a very simple way – after a method quite common in the anthracite coal mines. A perpendicular shaft or hole was made from the mine to the surface at a point inside of the Union rifle pits. A small furnace, or fire-place, was built at the bottom of this hole, or shaft, for the purpose of heating the air, and a fire was kept constantly burning, thus creating a draft. A door made of canvas was placed in the gallery, a little outside of this fire-place, thus shutting it in and shielding it from the outside air at the mouth of the mine. Wooden pipes, extending from the outside of this canvas door, along the gallery to the inner end thereof, conducted the fresh air to the point of operations, which,

Both main illustrated newspapers published retrospective engravings showing the Union mining operation at Petersburg. The front page of *Frank Leslie's Illustrated Newspaper* on August 20, 1864 **(a)** showed volunteers of the 48th Pennsylvania working by candlelight at the tunnel face. One man wields a makeshift pickaxe while the other two shovel soil into empty cracker boxes ready for shipping out of the mineshaft. An engraving which appeared in *Harper's Weekly* on the same date **(b)** captioned "Col. Pleasants superintending the arrival of the powder," was accompanied by a report from the artist, Alfred Waud, stating, "The mine being less than four feet in height, it was necessary to bend double in order to pass through it; the atmosphere was insufferably hot, and the ground so slippery as to quickly tire any one not used to such locomotion. Sitting at the end of it, the men passing in powder as silently as possible, speaking in low tones, and lighted by dimly burning dark lanterns, a queer sensation was felt on learning that not more than twelve or fourteen feet separated you from the rebel works in the earth-works overhead – an effect heightened by the sounds of the rebel workmen countermining, whose blows in faint thuds reached the ear." (Author's collection)

after supplying the miners with pure air, returned along the gallery towards the entrance of the mine, and, being stopped by the canvas door, the vitiated air moved into the furnace and up the shaft to the surface. By this means a constant current of air circulated through the gallery. As the work advanced, the inside end of the wooden pipe was extended so as to carry good air up to the face of the workings."

The need to keep the fire going constantly caused another problem, since its smoke might alert the Confederates to the mining operation. Thus, other fires were kept burning so that the smoke being emitted from the ventilation hole looked nothing out of the ordinary. A further difficulty was encountered on July 2, when the miners struck a thick layer of clay or marl. As a result, work slowed down considerably as the diggers chiselled away at the putty-like material. To overcome this problem, Pleasants ordered his men to tunnel upward at an incline until they encountered the extent of the marl layer. He then required them to resume digging on a level plane.

A constant fear for the miners was detection. As they approached their designated target beneath the enemy works, extreme care had to be taken to reduce the noise generated by tunneling. As a result, support timbers were notched outside the tunnel so they could be quietly wedged into place once carried in. There was also the possibility that information about the tunnel might reach the Confederates via word of mouth. Thus, the men involved in the operation were sworn to secrecy and ordered not to reveal the plan to their comrades or the folks at home via letter. To help preserve secrecy, IX Corps troops were ordered to keep up a continuous fire on the enemy line in their sector in order to keep the possibility of fraternization with the enemy to a minimum. Regardless of this, rumors did circulate among the ranks of

Based on an original sketch by Alfred Waud, this engraving illustrates how the 48th Pennsylvania hid from Confederate observers the powder kegs they shipped into the mine by carrying them in sandbags. (Courtesy of the National Park Service)

the Union troops, some of which claimed it was intended to blow up the whole of Petersburg. Inevitably, these stories were communicated to the Confederates via boasts and taunts of pickets, while some Union deserters told the enemy about the mine but provided insufficient information to permit the defending garrison to detect its exact location.

By July 17, 1864, the miners had dug a tunnel 510 feet long which had reached its destination under the Confederate defense works. At this stage, Pleasants ordered a temporary halt to work after information was received that the enemy suspected what the Yankees were up to. However, although a countermine was under way, it never came close to detecting the true location of the Union mine. Assured that they remained undetected, the Union miners next dug galleries to the left and right of the main tunnel. The former was extended to 37 feet, while the latter was dug to a distance of 38 feet. Eight chambers, or magazines, were incorporated into these for placing the powder charges.

The mine was complete and ready for the placement of the charge by July 23, and Meade was notified. There next followed a dispute between Burnside and Meade over the size of charge to be used. Experienced in the use of gunpowder as one-time proprietor of the Burnside Arms Company, Burnside requested the use of 12,000 pounds of explosive material. Several fellow officers felt differently, and advised Meade that a charge of that size might endanger Union troops in the adjacent works. Meade decided that only 8,000 pounds of powder should be used. Despite protests from Burnside, who maintained that 12,000 pounds would create a crater easier for assault troops to capture and pass through, Meade would not be swayed, and the designated charge remained at 8,000 pounds.

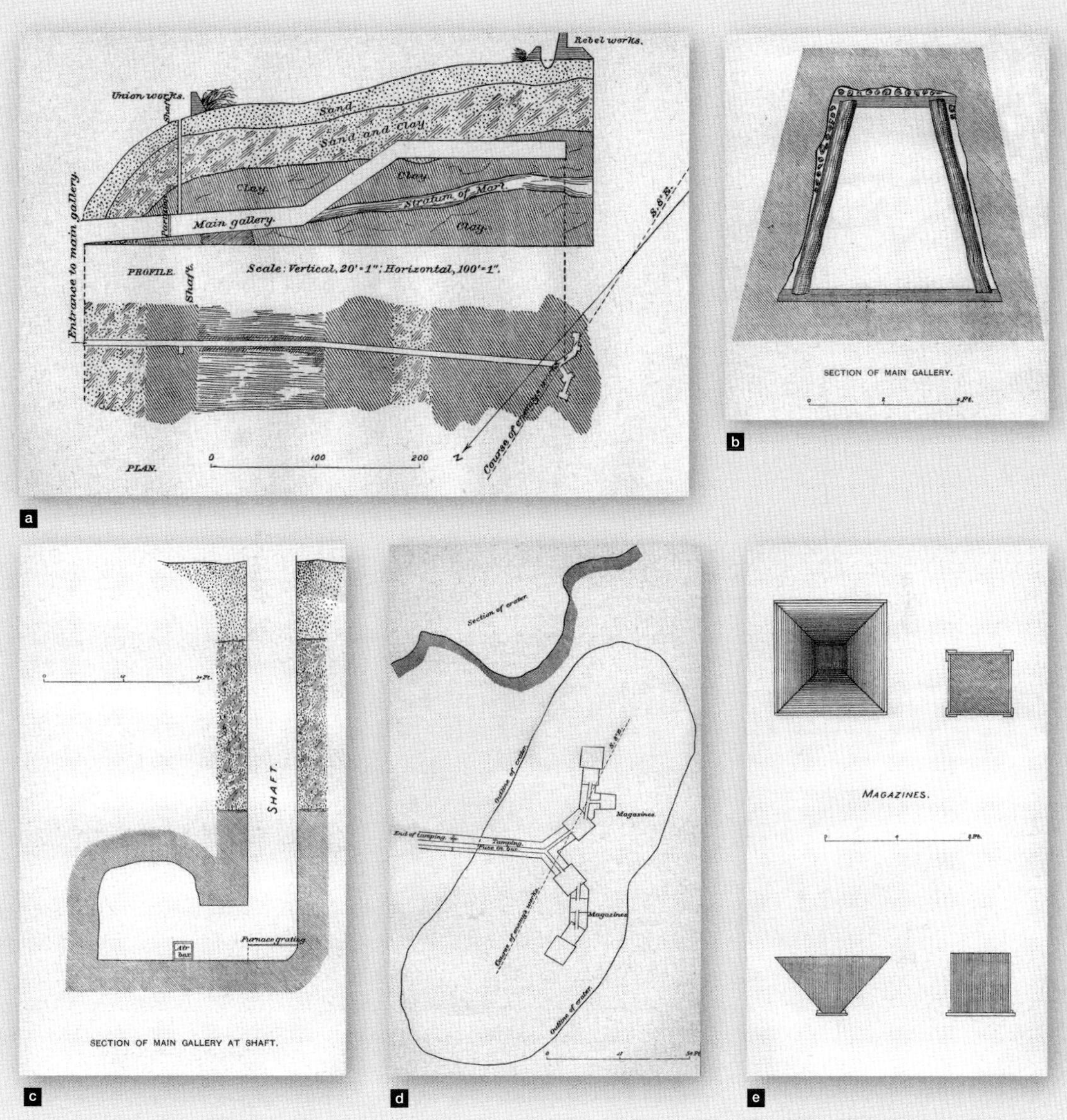

Accompanying the official report of Lieutenant Colonel Henry Pleasants dated August 2, 1864, this series of engravings, after drawings prepared by that officer, show detailed aspects of the Petersburg mining operation. **(a)** The cross section of the entire main gallery indicates the change of course made on July 2 after the miners encountered a thick layer of clay or marl. **(b)** The cross section detail shows the notched timbers used to support the roof and sides of the main gallery. Pleasants noted in his report, "The work progressed rapidly until the 2d of July, when it reached an extremely wet ground; the timbers gave way and the gallery nearly collapsed, the roof and floor of the mine nearly meeting. Retimbered it and started again." **(c)** Based on techniques employed in coal mining, fresh air was channelled into the main gallery along a six-inch square wooden tube, while foul air was drawn out via a vertical shaft with a constantly burning fire at its base. The furnace grating, air box and shaft are shown in this drawing. **(d)** Note the extent of the crater caused by the explosion in this plan of the lateral galleries. According to Pleasants' report, "The charge consisted of 320 kegs of powder, each containing about twenty-five pounds. It was placed in eight magazines connected with each other by troughs half filled with powder. These troughs from the lateral galleries met at the inner end of the main one, and from this point I had three lines of fuses for a distance of ninety-eight feet." **(e)** Plans showing one of the eight six-foot square, funnel-shaped magazines used to hold the 8,000 pounds of powder used in the mine explosion. (Author's collection)

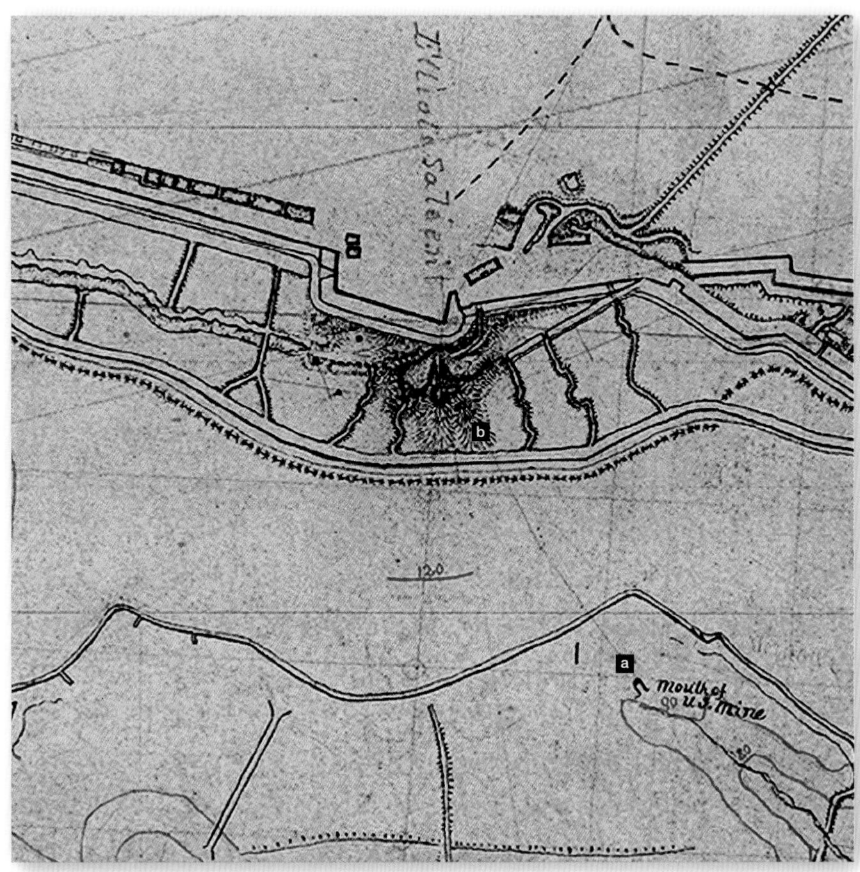

The course of the tunnelling from the mouth of the mine to Elliott's Salient is indicated on this 1865 map by a faint pencil line (a–b). (Author's collection)

PLANNING FOR THE BATTLE

As the mining operation neared its conclusion, and seemingly against all the odds, Burnside realized a plan was needed for an assault after detonation of the explosives. His choice to spearhead the attack was the Fourth Division, IX Corps, commanded by Brigadier General Edward Ferrero. Born in Spain to Italian parents, Ferrero was a colourful character and the subject of much derision among fellow officers for having been a dancing instructor before the war. His division consisted of two brigades of African-American troops recently recruited in Maryland, Ohio, Pennsylvania and Connecticut to make up Burnside's corps. Not actively engaged after Grant and the Army of the Potomac moved south of the James, the Fourth had been charged with the duties of guarding ammunition trains and serving as a labour force for almost the entire army since its arrival in Virginia. For example, the records of Company B, 43rd USCT for June of that year stated: "Followed in the rear of the Army doing picket duty and guarding wagon trains until the Army crossed the James River on June 18. Since that time the company has been engaged in throwing up entrenchments, building forts, and doing picket duty on the flanks of the Army."

Ferrero prepared and trained his division for the attack as best he could, and was advised by subordinate officers that they were confident the African-American troops would give a good account of themselves. Brigadier General Henry G. Thomas, commanding the 2nd Brigade, recorded, "We were all pleased with the compliment of being chosen to lead the assault. Both officers

Born in Spain in 1831, Edward Ferrero ran a dancing school established by his father in New York City before the Civil War, and was also active in the state militia, commanding the 51st Regiment by 1861. He led his regiment at Roanoke Island and New Bern through 1861–62, and was promoted to command the 2nd Brigade, 2nd Division, North Carolina in April, receiving the rank of brigadier general in September, 1862. Transferring west, he was given charge of the 2nd Brigade, 2nd Division, Army of the Ohio, and by August 1863 commanded the First Division, IX Corps, Army of the Ohio. He returned east in April 1864 in time to lead the newly recruited African-American Fourth Division, IX Corps, at Petersburg. (Library of Congress LC-B811-3333B)

and men were eager to show the white troops what the colored division could do. We had acquired confidence in our men. They believed us infallible. We had drilled certain movements, to be executed in gaining and occupying the crest. It is an axiom in military art that there are times when the ardour, hopefulness, and enthusiasm of new troops, not yet rendered doubtful by reverses or chilled by defeat, more than compensate, in a dash, for training and experience."

Burnside ordered Ferrero and his brigade commanders to the advanced trenches to locate areas where he could concentrate his force and inspect the ground it would have to cross during the attack. The resulting plan as devised by Ferrero in consultation with Burnside consisted of a lightning thrust by a tight column of two brigades which would approach the front line via covered ways and after deployment debouch from the trenches to force a breach through the crater created by the explosion. This formation would then undertake a complicated maneuver in which the regiment at the head of the right brigade would wheel to the right to drive out the Confederate forces to the north, while its counterpart leading the left brigade would perform the same task to the south. The remainder of the column would drive on to capture the high ground behind the Confederate line, which consisted of a rise about 400 yards to the northeast and close to the small township of Blandford. On the summit of this hill was a small brick-built church with a cemetery, which gave it the name "Cemetery Hill" in subsequent battle reports. Once in possession of this key ground, with support from other divisions of the corps, the African-American Fourth Division would sweep on to capture Petersburg itself.

Meanwhile, the Union high command dithered regarding whether the attack should go ahead or not. By the end of July 1864 Meade considered the mine explosion and ensuing infantry assault to be the best hope of a breakthrough. Earlier in the month, he had preferred a plan by General John G. Barnard, Chief Engineer of the Armies in the field on Grant's staff, to target the Confederate trenches in front of Warren's V Corps line, employing a mass attack preceded by a bombardment of 100 guns. When this plan failed to develop, he reluctantly decided to support Burnside's mine assault.

James Hewitt Ledlie was a civil engineer before the Civil War. Born in New York in 1832, he was commissioned a major in the 3rd New York Artillery on May 22, 1861, and was promoted to lieutenant colonel and colonel respectively on September 28 and December 23, 1861. Receiving the rank of Brigadier General, USV, on December 24, 1862, he became Chief of Artillery under Major General John G. Foster, Department of North Carolina. With the expiration of his commission in March 1863, he was re-appointed in October of that year and given command of the First Division, IX Corps on June 9, 1864. Following his failure in command during the Battle of the Crater, Grant described him in his *Memoirs* as "being otherwise inefficient, proved also to possess disqualification less common among soldiers". Ledlie resigned his commission on January 23, 1865, and resumed his career as a successful civil engineer. (US National Archives NWDNS-111-B-4461)

However, relationships quickly deteriorated between the two officers. Burnside was Meade's senior in rank and in 1862 had held his post in command of the Army of the Potomac. While Burnside accepted the situation, Meade was not so agreeable or courteous. Matters deteriorated when Burnside requested command of forces supporting the IX Corps during the assault. Meade rejected this request outright, believing that Burnside was overstepping his authority. Meade next meddled with Burnside's attack plan, which was modified at the last minute. In a meeting with Grant, Meade suggested that if the African-American division led the attack and it failed, it would give the impression that they were being used as "cannon fodder." Such criticism had been the case when the 54th Massachusetts spearheaded the unsuccessful attack on Battery Wagner, in Charleston Harbor, on July 18, 1863. In his after-battle report, Brigadier General R.S. Ripley, the Confederate commanding officer of the fort, had stated, "The enemy had put the poor negroes, whom they had forced into an unnatural service, in front, to be slaughtered." Indeed, Grant recalled later of the decision made at the last minute on July 28, 1864, "General Meade said that if we put the colored troops in front (we had only one division) and it should prove a failure, it would then be said, and very properly, that we were shoving these people ahead to get killed because we did not care anything about them. But that could not be said if we put white troops in front."

Inexcusably, Burnside only learned of the change of plan at about 11 a.m. on the day before the attack, when Meade arrived at his headquarters accompanied by General Edward O.C. Ord, and informed him that Grant had concurred with his opinion. Requested to replace the force trained to make the initial assault, Burnside overcame his anger and disappointment, and acquiesced graciously stating, "Very well, General, I will carry out this plan to the best of my ability." The troops now designated to lead the attack would have to come from his three battle-weary white divisions. Unable to make a clear choice, and, to his detriment thereafter, Burnside asked the three divisional commanders concerned to draw lots, and Brigadier General James H. Ledlie, commanding the First Division, drew the short straw.

On paper, Robert B. Potter and Orlando Willcox were the more experienced generals, while Ledlie was the most recent arrival to the IX Corps. In fact, he was the worst possible choice to lead what could potentially have been one of the most critical charges of the war. While the troops under his command had acquitted themselves with bravery during the fighting at Petersburg on June 17, and in an unauthorized attack on Confederate fortifications at Ox Ford on July 26, Ledlie was drunk on both occasions, and was seemingly incapable of going into combat without being inebriated. To his credit, Burnside was unaware of these failings. However, Grant was well aware of them, having been responsible for transferring Ledlie to the Army of the Potomac from North Carolina on June 9, 1864. For whatever reason, Grant did not share this knowledge with Meade, Burnside, or anyone else, until after the assault on the crater.

Meade issued orders for the IX Corps to be massed for the attack during the early hours of July 30, 1864. Burnside was advised to have the trenches to his front cleared of obstructions so that his troops could quickly debouch. However, he did not follow this advice as it would serve as a warning to the Confederates that an attack was imminent. Pioneer units armed with axes and spades were to lead the way clearing abatis and wire entanglements from the path of the advancing troops. The V and XVIII Corps were readied to

Some of the 5,000 troops of the Union V Corps who took part in the attack await orders to advance in support of the IX Corps following the detonation of the mine on July 30, 1864. (Author's collection)

follow up the initial assault, which was to commence with the detonation of the mine at 3.30 a.m. At that time, Ledlie's division would burst through the resulting crater and make for Cemetery Hill, while Willcox would advance to protect his right flank and Potter would perform the same duty on his left. Ferrero's African-American division now had the task of waiting in reserve until the other divisions had cleared the way, after which they would follow Ledlie's path and possibly occupy Blandford.

Once the matter of which troops were to spearhead the attack was settled, there remained the problem of concentrating the thousands of men needed on too small a space of ground in preparation for zero hour. By 9 a.m. on July 29, elements of the IX Corps began to form in the trenches and covered ways opposite Cemetery Hill. According to Major Charles Houghton, 14th New York Heavy Artillery, the rank and file understood the importance of the work ahead: "The men were cautioned to prevent the rattling of tin cups and bayonets, because we were so near the enemy that they would discover our movements. We marched with the stillness of death; not a word was said above a whisper. We knew, of course, that something very important was to be done and that we were to play a prominent part." Waiting in the trenches occupied by the 3rd New Hampshire, Captain Eldridge J. Copp noted, "Daylight approaches, and yet no sound except the usual firing upon the picket line in our front, and on along the whole line to our left until the sounds are lost in the distant." Still standing after hours, some officers permitted their men to lie down, and many fell into a fitful slumber. By 3.30 a.m. Ledlie's division was in place, with the Second Brigade, commanded by Colonel Elisha G. Marshall, in front, and that of General William F. Bartlett ready to follow up behind it. Daylight came slowly, and still they waited with nerves strained as they prepared to move forward when the order was given.

The Confederate line opposite the IX Corps was held by the division of Major General Bushrod Johnson, with Ransom's North Carolina brigade, commanded by Colonel Lee McAfee, to the north. A South Carolina brigade commanded by Colonel Stephen Elliott stood at the centre, while Wise's Virginia brigade under Colonel Thomas J. Goode, manned the trenches to the south. Elliott's South Carolinians were posted around the salient under which the mine was dug, with the 26th, 17th, 18th, 22nd and 23rd regiments arranged from left to right. Five companies of the 22nd South Carolina, manned the actual salient, with the 17th and 28th South Carolina to their left and the remainder of the 22nd, 18th and 23rd South Carolina to their right. A battery composed of four Napoleon 12-pounders was also situated in the fort, manned by the Virginia battery of Captain Richard G. Pegram.

THE ASSAULT BEGINS

As dawn approached, the massed formations consisting of about 9,000 men of the IX Corps, supported by 8,000 troops with the XVIII Corps, a further 5,000 in the V Corps, and a division of the X Corps, awaited the signal to begin the attack. Burnside arrived at his advanced headquarters, known as the "Fourteen Gun Battery," or Fort Morton (after engineer officer Major James St Clair Morton killed on June 17 near that location), at about 2 a.m. About 600 yards behind the centre of the IX Corps lines, it provided a good view of the ground over which the action would take place. Meade and staff occupied Burnside's regular headquarters at about 3.15 a.m., and shortly before the scheduled detonation of the mine. Situated centrally with good telegraphic communications, it was about a mile from the trenches where the IX Corps was massing, and nothing could be seen of what would take place in the Crater from that point.

The electromagnetic telegraph had been developed by Samuel Morse during the 1840s, and had become a vital aspect of the communication system of the US Signal Corps since June 1861. Its correct use during the action that followed might have produced a model example of post-Napoleonic warfare. However, this turned out not to be the case. Although Meade used the telegraph to continually request updates on the progress of proceedings leading to the attack, Burnside consistently refused to respond. As a result, what could have helped achieve victory simply exacerbated the tension between the two commanders.

As Meade set out for Burnside's HQ, he had a telegraphic message relayed to Burnside stating that, due to the extreme darkness of the early morning, he could delay the detonation of the mine until it became lighter. In disagreement with this decision, Burnside failed to send a reply via the telegraphic operator in Fort Morton, and went ahead with the original plan and timing. But as the minutes ticked by, and the deadline for detonation passed and nothing happened, Burnside remained impossible to contact. Believing at first that the delay was caused by a miscalculation in the timing of the fuse, he dispatched an aide-de-camp to the mineshaft to establish the cause. Meanwhile, Meade became increasingly concerned at the lack of communication. Joined by Grant, he also sent an aide to Burnside to find out what was going on, but the aide did not find his way back. Finally, at 4.15 a.m., Meade used the telegraphic wire again to send a message urgently requesting a reason for the delay. As there was nothing to report, Burnside again did not respond, and continued to ignore a further telegraphed dispatch to the same effect. Becoming infuriated at Burnside's stubborn refusal to take advantage of a state-of-the art communication system, Meade sent a further message stating that if the mine was not going to be detonated, he would make other arrangements for an attack anyway. Once again, Burnside refused to respond. At this point, Meade finally ordered a general assault, whether the

a b

Established on June 21, 1861, under A.J. Myer, the US Signal Corps was commanded by Colonel Anson Stager, a prewar general superintendent of the Western Union Telegraph Company, by 1864. If used properly, the military telegraph would have vastly improved communications between Meade and Burnside on July 30, 1864. These engravings (both of which are from the author's collection) were published in *Harper's Weekly* on January 24, 1863, and were accompanied by the following captions:

(a) The Army Telegraph – setting up the wire during an action.
"Of this important institution he [artist A.R. Waud] says: 'The army signal-telegraph has been so far perfected that in a few hours quite a large force can be in constant connection with head-quarters. This, while a battle is progressing, is a great convenience. The wire used is a copper one insulated, raised on light poles, made expressly for the purpose, on convenient trees, or trailed along fences. The wire and the instrument can be easily carried in a cart, which as it proceeds unwinds the wire, and, when a connection is made, becomes the telegraph-office. Where the cart cannot go the men carry the drum of wire by hand. In the picture the cart has come to a halt, and the signal-men are hastening along – some with the drum, while others with crow-bars make the holes for the poles, upon which it is rapidly raised.

(b) The operator at work.
"The machine is a simple one, worked by a handle, which is passed around a dial-plate marked with numerals and the alphabet. By stopping at the necessary letters a message is easily spelled out upon the instrument at the other end of the line, which repeats by a pointer every move on the dial-plate. The whole thing is so simple that any man able to read and write can work it with facility.'"

mine was detonated or not. Meanwhile, Burnside was at last informed by a staff officer that the mine's fuse had gone out, but had been re-lit and that the charge would be ignited any minute. In fact, Sergeant Reese (overseer of the mining) and Lieutenant Jacob Douty, Company K, 48th Pennsylvania, had bravely entered the mine, discovered the problem and remedied it.

At about 4.45 a.m. there was a dull roar, and soil and smoke belched forth from the ground where the Confederate earthworks once stood. Lieutenant J.J. Chase, 32nd Maine, was asleep when the explosion occurred and recalled, "suddenly I was awakened. Oh horrors! Was I in the midst of an earthquake? Was the ground around me about to part and let me into the bowels of the earth. Hardly realizing where I was or what it all meant, this terrible thunder, accompanied by the upheaving and rocking of the ground, springing to my feet I recovered my senses enough to understand that an explosion had taken place. Glancing in the direction of Cemetery Hill, I beheld a huge mass of earth being thrown up, followed by a dark lurid cloud of smoke." According to aide-de-camp Major William H. Powell, 4th US Infantry, "It was a magnificent spectacle, and as the mass of earth went up into the air, carrying with it men, guns, carriages, and timbers, and spread out like an immense cloud as it reached its altitude, so close were the Union lines that the mass appeared as if it would descend immediately upon the troops waiting to make

ABOVE LEFT
Inscribed on the reverse side "Petersburg Mine, Va./July 30, 1864/23d U.S. colored/18th U.S.," this pencil and Chinese white drawing is accompanied by the following on-the-spot description by artist Alfred Waud: "The advance to the 'crater' after the explosion of the mine. In the middle distance are the mounds of earth thrown up by the explosion: beyond upon the high ground cemetery hill the Confederates' inner line of works, which if they had carried, would have given the Union Army Petersburg and Richmond. In the foreground troops are seen advancing to and beyond Burnside's outer intrenched [sic] line and moving upon the Confederate defenses. These were – on the left Bartlett's Massachusetts brigade, and on the right, the Negro troops – this sketch was made about 8 AM July 30th 1864." (Library of Congress LC-USZC4-10794)

ABOVE RIGHT
Entitled "Charge of the 2nd Division, 9th Army Corps, into the Crater," this depiction of an eyewitness sketch by artist Andrew McCallum, was accompanied by a report stating that the assault was made "bravely, but from faults which the court of enquiry will explain, time had been lost, officers were absent, and the result was a sad slaughter of men whom the country cannot afford to lose." (Author)

the charge. This caused them to break and scatter to the rear, and about ten minutes were consumed in re-forming for the attack. Not much was lost by this delay, however, as it took nearly that time for the cloud of dust to pass off. The order was then given for the advance."

The first Union troops to move forward were the Second Brigade, First Division, XVIII Corps, the first line of battle being composed of the 2nd Provisional Pennsylvania Heavy Artillery, commanded by Lieutenant Colonel Benjamin G. Barney. The second line consisted of the 14th New York Artillery, under Captain Lorenzo I. Jones. Following up in a third line of battle was the 3rd Maryland Battalion, led by Lieutenant Colonel Gilbert P. Robinson, and the 179th New York Volunteers, with Major John Barton at their head. As no part of the Union line of breastworks had been removed, these men clambered over them as best they could. This in itself broke up the ranks, but they did not stop to re-form and pushed ahead toward the crater, which was about 130 yards distant. As debris from the explosion had covered up the abatis and chevaux-de-frise in front of the enemy works, passage across no man's land was rendered less difficult.

These men little anticipated what they would see upon arrival at the crater left by the explosion. An enormous hole about 30 feet deep, 60 feet wide and 170 feet long, was filled with dust, chunks of clay, gun tubes, broken carriages, projecting timbers and men buried in various ways – some up to their necks, others to their waists, and some with only their feet and legs protruding from the earth. Half the Confederate salient had been destroyed. About 350 men were killed or wounded by the explosion. Two of the 12-pounder Napoleons had been hurled into the ground in front of the Union lines. The remaining two guns still stood in the southern part of the earthwork, which survived the destruction. In total, the 22nd South Carolina sustained an immediate loss of 170 killed and wounded. The 18th South Carolina lost 43 killed and 43 wounded; the 17th South Carolina, 25 killed and 8 wounded; and the 23rd South Carolina, 14 killed and 41 wounded. Pegram's battery suffered 22 killed and wounded.

Having advanced with the Pennsylvanians, Major William recalled the arrival of Union troops at the resulting crater: "The whole scene of the explosion struck every one dumb with astonishment as we arrived at the crest of the debris. It was impossible for the troops of the Second Brigade to move forward in line, as they had advanced; and, owing to the broken state they were in, every man crowding up to look into the hole, and being pressed by the First Brigade, which was immediately in rear, it was equally impossible to

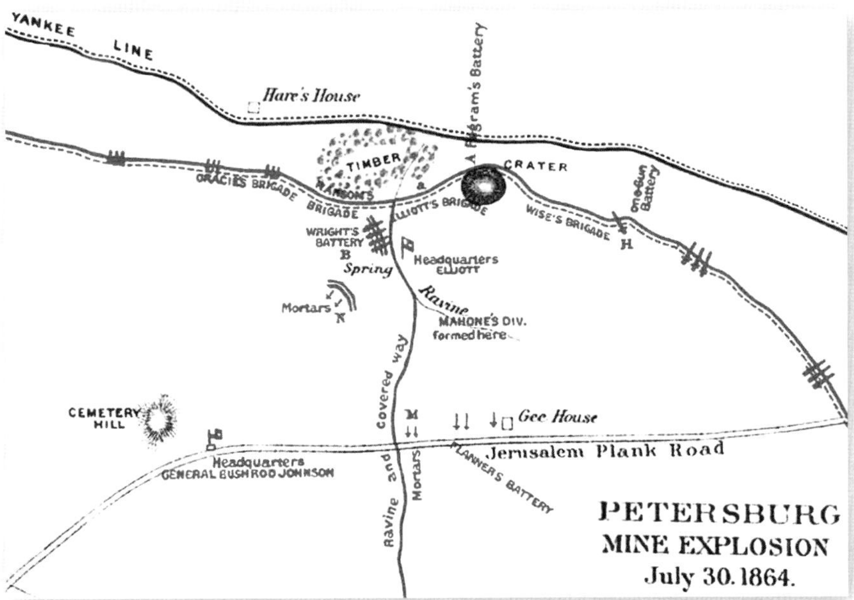

TOP LEFT
This watercolor was based on a sketch made by Alfred Waud in the trenches of the V Corps, and shows the moment of the mine explosion. The bearded officer in the foreground watching through field glasses is Major James Duane, Chief Engineer of the Army of the Potomac, and the others represent his staff officers. (Courtesy of the National Park Service)

BOTTOM LEFT
This map from the *Official Military Atlas of the Civil War* shows the deployment of Confederate troops and location of their commanders and artillery during the battle. (Author's collection)

move by the flank, by any command, around the crater. Before the brigade commanders could realize the situation, the two brigades became inextricably mixed, in the desire to look into the hole."

Despite the confusion in and around the Crater, Colonel Marshall yelled to his brigade to move forward, and the men obeyed, jumping, sliding, and tumbling into the huge gaping hole, and scrambling over the debris, and dead and dying men. They were followed by General Bartlett's First Brigade of Massachusetts men. Meanwhile, on the other side of the crater the leading members of the Second Brigade attempted unsuccessfully to climb up and over the rim. In doing so, many were killed by musket shots from the rear, fired by the Confederates who still occupied the traverses and entrenchments to the right and left of the Crater.

Arriving with Bartlett's brigade, and in command of the 56th Massachusetts, Colonel Stephen M. Weld, Jr later recorded, "Here, in the crater, was a confused mob of men continually increasing by fresh arrivals. Of course, nothing could be seen from this crater of the situation of affairs around us. Any attempt to move forward from this crater was absolutely hopeless. The men could not be got forward. It was a perfect mob, as far as any company or regimental organization was concerned, and that necessarily from the way we went forward, and not from any fault of the officers or men. To ask men to go forward in such a condition was useless. Each one felt as if he were to encounter the whole Confederate force alone and unsupported. The moral backing of an organized body of men, which each would sustain his companions on either side, was wanting."

Meanwhile, the Confederate survivors were initially in a state of shock. Commanding the 17th South Carolina and Evan's Brigade after the wounding of Stephen Elliott, Colonel Fitz William McMaster recalled, "For some minutes there was the utmost consternation among our men. Some scampered out of the lines; some, paralyzed with fear, vaguely scratched at the counter-scarp as if trying to escape. Smoke and dust filled the air." Colonel David G. Fleming, commanding the 23rd South Carolina, was blown up by the explosion. Command of both the 22nd and 23rd South Carolina devolved upon Captain Joseph N. Shedd, Company E of the former regiment, who by "his coolness and intrepidity," rallied some of the survivors. According to Union Major Powell, one of the Confederates pulled out of the exploded earth after the arrival of Ledlie's division proved to be "a second lieutenant [William H. Scott] of the battery which had been blown up. The fresh air revived him, and he was soon able to walk and talk. He was very grateful and said that he was asleep when the explosion took place, and only awoke to find himself wriggling up in the air; then a few seconds afterward he felt himself descending, and soon lost consciousness."

Regaining their senses, many South Carolinians manned what remained of the earthworks and put up a defensive fire. According to McMaster, "they began to cheer, and our men bounded on the banquette and commenced firing on the ranks of men who were rushing in without firing a gun. By this some

Several sketches produced by eyewitnesses captured the death and destruction following the detonation of the Petersburg mine. **LEFT** This detail from the work of *Frank Leslie's* artist E.F. Mullen shows one of the huge chunks of clay hurled into the air by the explosion. **RIGHT** Commanding a Confederate artillery battalion near Elliott's Salient, Major James C. Coit made this sketch while burying the dead of the Crater battle under a flag of truce. (Author's collection)

of the men of the gallant Eighteenth, who extricated themselves from the bank which covered them, came rushing down the trenches, and as many as could picked up guns and began firing. For a considerable time the firing was done entirely by the infantry."

South of the Crater Major Wade Gibbs, a determined artillery officer, gathered enough willing hands together to work a gun from Davidson's battery which had been abandoned after the explosion. At a range of 1,000 feet this single piece soon began to cause havoc among the Union troops clinging to the southern edge of the crater.

Not all the Union troops were phased by the surrounding chaos. A detachment of the 14th New York Artillery under Sergeant Wesley Stanley, Company D, seized the two Confederate cannon remaining after the explosion and turned them on their assailants to the south. Other groups of men began to dig in. Armed with Model 1860 Spencer repeating rifles, Company K, 57th Massachusetts, commanded by Captain Benjamin A. Spear, also harassed the enemy artillery in their front. First Sergeant Barnard A. Strasbaugh, Company A, 3rd Maryland Battalion, led another squad of sharpshooters armed with this weapon. During the confused fighting, he single-handedly captured eight Confederate prisoners. For this action, and for recapturing the flag of the 2nd Pennsylvania Heavy Artillery, he was awarded the Medal of Honor. However, these tactics merely exacerbated the situation, as the main objective of the first two brigades of assault troops was to press on and capture Cemetery Hill beyond.

In the absence of any divisional leadership, brigade and regimental commanders attempted to salvage the situation. The 179th New York and 3rd Maryland Battalion tried unsuccessfully to push into the hanging Confederate flank to the north. The 2nd Pennsylvania Heavy Artillery advanced the farthest west, reaching just beyond the edge of the crater. Meanwhile, the attack of the 3rd Division north of the Crater and that of the 2nd Division to its south were both stalled, as they were dependent on Ledlie's division acting as a spearhead for the whole operation.

Meanwhile, about half an hour after the mine detonation, Ledlie took shelter in a bombproof being used as a dressing station about 55 yards to the rear of the Union front line, where he plied himself with rum borrowed from an army surgeon. When Major Powell arrived later to advise his commander that his troops either side of the hole created by the explosion would need to be cleared as they were being pushed back into the mass of the 1st Division struggling in the crater, he repeated an earlier order directing them to "advance on Cemetery Hill." Joined soon after by Ferrero, who also imbibed from the rum jug, Ledlie received an order from Burnside stating: "The general wishes you to move your troops forward to the crest of the hill and hold it." In response, Ledlie sent an aide into the crater to pass on the order. There next came an order for Ferrero to "move his division through and charge down to the city," to which he responded cryptically – he would do so "as soon as those troops were out of the way." After receiving a second and third order to the same effect, Ferrero left the bombproof accompanied by Ledlie to at last carry out the command. Placed at his disposal as an adviser, Colonel William W. Loring, Inspector General on the staff of Burnside, next insisted that Ferrero wait while he sought out the IX Corps commander to inform him of the true situation, and that sending the African-American division into the crater would only add to an already hopeless situation. Loring returned shortly after to inform Ferrero that the order was peremptory.

Commanding the First Brigade, First Division, IX Army Corps, during the disastrous assault on the Crater in July 1864, General William Francis Bartlett (1840–76) was a student at Harvard when he enlisted as a private in the 4th Massachusetts Volunteers in 1861. Commissioned a captain in the 20th Massachusetts Infantry, he lost a leg at Yorktown in early 1862. Following recovery, he received the colonelcy of the 49th Massachusetts in November 1862 and took part in the capture of Fort Hudson in July, 1863. Receiving a less severe wound at the Wilderness in May, 1864, he was able to accept a brigade command. After having his cork leg shot away in the Crater, he asked to be lifted up in order to see the approach of Sander's Confederate brigade, whereupon he was hit by a ball which badly gashed his scalp. Taken prisoner and placed in Libby Prison, he was returned north as part of a prisoner exchange, and placed in command of the IX Corps, which he led with distinction until the end of the war. For gallant and meritorious services, he was breveted Major General of US Volunteers on March 13, 1865. (US National Archive NWDNS-111-B-4591)

Published as a set on the front cover of *Frank Leslie's* on August 27, 1864, these engravings were entitled "Incidents in the battle of Petersburg after the explosion of the Mine." **(a)** Some Confederates showed compassion and carried water to fallen Union soldiers holding up a canteen as a "flag of truce." **(b)** Captioned "Come Yanks, for God's sake take me out of this place! It is all over now, and there's no use letting a fellow stick here," this engraving shows Union troops rescuing a Rebel half buried by the mine detonation. This was probably inspired by the rescue of Second Lieutenant William H. Scott of Pegram's battery. **(c)** Several Union regiments, including the 29th USCT, managed to plant their colors on the opposite rim of the Crater, as shown in this depiction of the battle. **(d)** With varying success, many Union wounded attempted to cross back over to their own entrenchments during the battle. (Author's collection)

The Fourth Division finally received the order to charge at about 7.30 a.m. The First Brigade, under Colonel Joshua K. Sigfried, went forward first, followed by the Second Brigade led by Henry G. Thomas. Watching from his trench sector Captain James H. Clark, 115th New York, reported: "A colored division mount the works, and they too go forward on the charge. We watch eagerly, it is their first fight and we wonder if they will stand the shock. Noble fellows! Grandly they cross the field; they are under a qithering [sic] fire, but still rush on regardless of fallen comrades, and the storm of pitiless lead and relentless grape that pours upon them three sides, and gain the works with a ringing cheer."

According to the battle report of Colonel Sigfried, great difficulty was then experienced passing through the crater, "owing to its crowded condition – living, wounded, dead, and dying crowded so thickly." But make their way they did. The 43rd USCT then rose up and charged over the crest of the crater, reaching the Confederate support line trenches. There they captured a number of prisoners, a "rebel stand of colors," and re-captured a "stand of national

Based on an oil painting by John Elder, which was commissioned by William Mahone in 1869, this steel plate engraving depicts the 12th Virginia leading the charge into the Crater during the Confederate counterattack. The staff of the battle flag carried by this regiment was snapped in two during this action, but was quickly spliced back together with a ramrod and planted on the earthworks after the Confederates had reclaimed what remained of Elliott's Salient. (*Battles & Leaders*)

colors." However, the toll on officers and men was great. Colonel Delevan Bates, commanding the 13th USCT, fell shot through the face at the head of his regiment, for which he received a posthumous Medal of Honor. Major James C. Leeke, of the same regiment, stood on the ramparts urging his men forward with blood from a chest wound gushing from his mouth.

Colonel Henry G. Thomas, leading the Second Brigade, reported: "The instant I reached the First Brigade I attempted to charge, but the Thirty-first was disheartened at its loss of officers and could not be gotten out promptly. Captain [Marshall L.] Dempey and Lieutenant [Christopher] Pennell and myself then attempted to lead them, but the fire was so hot that half the few who came out of the works were shot. Here Lieutenant Pennell was killed and riddled through and through. He died with the flag in his hand, doing everything an officer could do to lead on the men ... Immediately after this I was ordered by Brigadier General Ferrero to advance in concert with Colonel Sigfried and take the crest. I ordered the Twenty-ninth this time to lead, which it did gallantly, closely followed by the Twenty-eighth and a few of the Twenty-third, when it was at once engaged by a heavy charging column of the enemy, and after a struggle driven back over our rifle-pits. At this moment a panic commenced. The black and white troops came pouring back together. A few, more gallant, than the rest, without organization, but guided by a soldier's instinct, remained on the side of the pits nearest our line and held the enemy at bay some ten or fifteen minutes, until they were nearly all shot away ... Whether we fought well or not, the scores of our dead lying thick as if mowed down by the hand of some mighty reaper and the terrible loss of officers can best attest."

THE CONFEDERATE COUNTERATTACK

In his headquarters at Dunn's Hill, Robert E. Lee was alerted to the desperate situation caused by the detonation of the Union mine by a staff officer sent by Beauregard, who had been awakened by the explosion in Petersburg. Lee immediately gave orders for two brigades of Anderson's division, 3rd Corps, commanded by Brigadier General William "Little Billy" Mahone, to reinforce Johnson's reeling troops. Posted at the Wilcox Farm near Lieutenant Creek

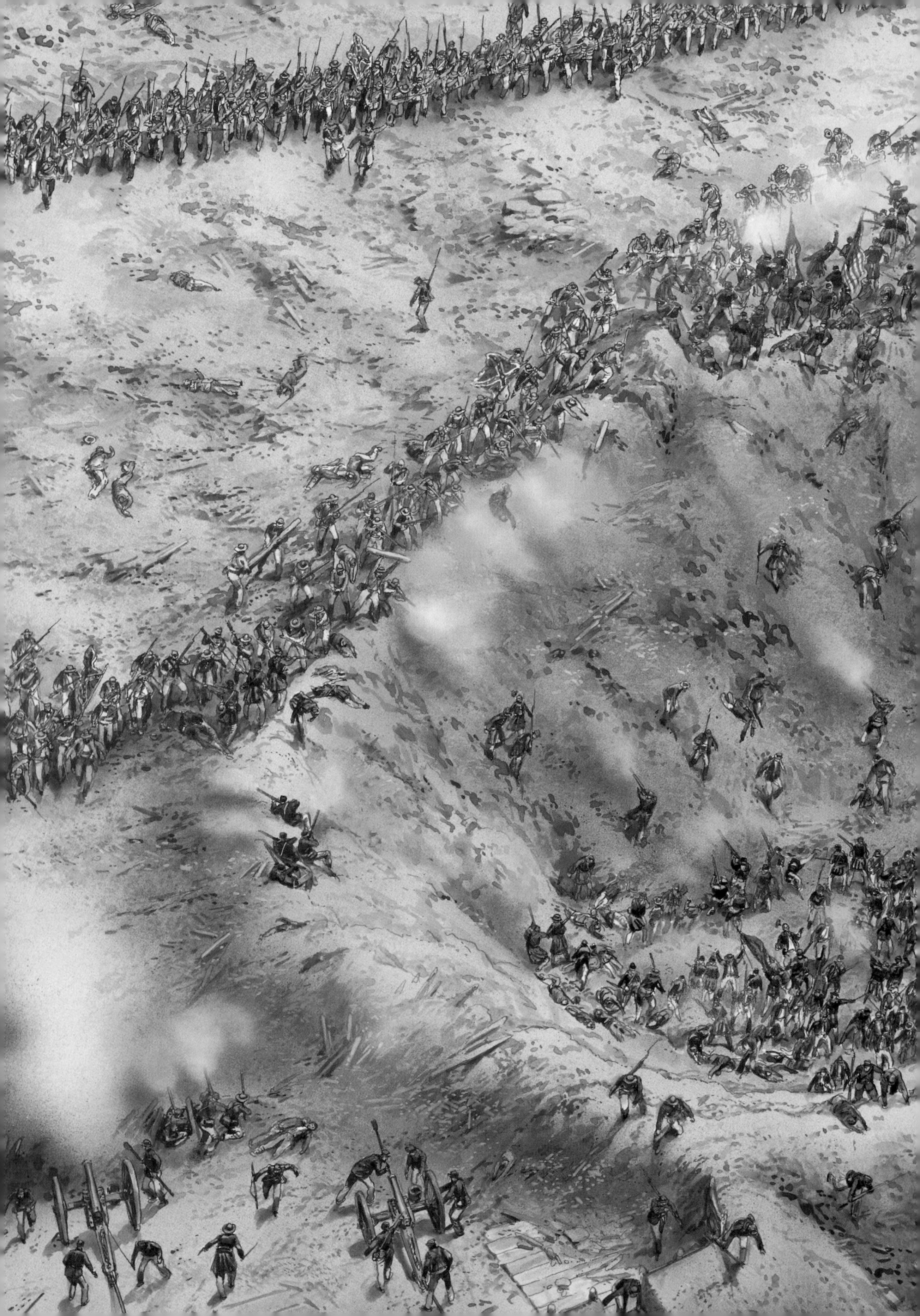

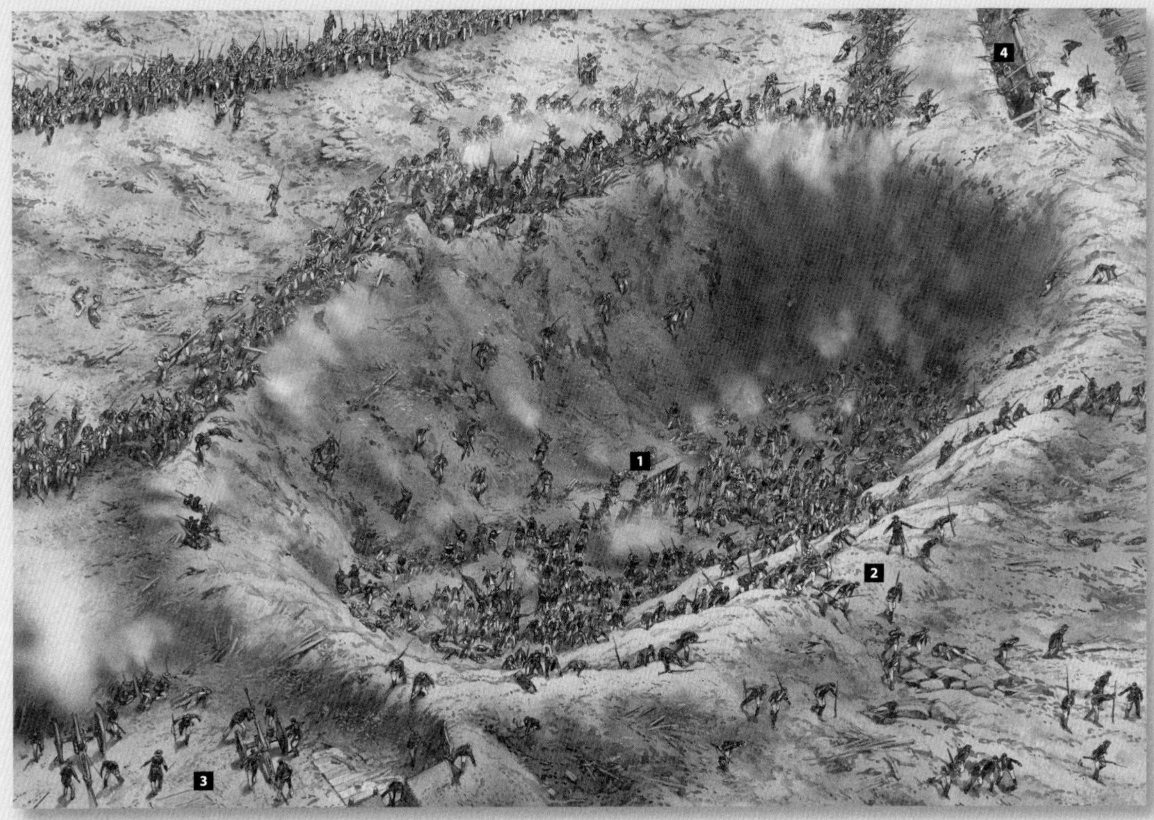

THE CRATER, JULY 30, 1864 (PP 54–55)

Toward the end of the hideous struggle in and around the Crater on July 30, 1864, Lee ordered two brigades of Anderson's division, under Brigadier General William "Little Billy" Mahone, to counterattack. The slaughter that ensued resulted in a defeat for the Union Army that cost 3,798 killed, wounded and missing of a total of 20,708 engaged in the mine assault. Confederate casualties probably amounted to about 1,500.

The Confederate counterattack is seen here moving in from the west. The Virginians formed the first wave, and the North Carolinians the second. As the Confederates prepared to charge, Lieutenant Colonel John A. Bross **(1)**, 29th USCT, rose up and, waving the regimental colors, urged his black troops on yelling, "Forward, my brave boys!" Inevitably, Bross was cut down before the remnants of his regiment could scramble out of the Crater.

The Confederates yelled "No quarter!" as they went in with fixed bayonets. At the moment they began their charge, the Union commanders in the Crater and nearby trenches received orders to retreat **(2)**, and had begun passing the order along the line as best they could. Hence, the battle-shocked Union troops offered only token resistance when the Confederates closed on them. Reaching the edge of the Crater, many Confederates fired at pointblank range while others hurled clods of earth, wood, discharged muskets, and loose cannonballs down at the terrified Union troops.

Captain John C. Featherston, Company F, 9th Alabama, observed, "There were quite a number of abandoned muskets with bayonets on them lying on the ground around the fort. Our men began pitching them over the embankment, bayonet foremost, trying to harpoon the men inside."

The presence of African-Americans incensed the Confederates. According to Featherston, "The enemy shrank back, and the death grapple continued until most of the Yankees found in there were killed. This slaughter would not have been so great had not our men found negro soldiers in the fort with the whites. This was the first time we had met negro troops, and the men were enraged at them for being there and at the whites for having them there." Many black troops were shot and bayoneted as they tried to surrender. Others were killed by their white Union comrades for fear of being murdered by the Confederates if caught with African-American soldiers.

Not all the Union troops were phased by the surrounding chaos. A detachment of the 14th New York Artillery under Sergeant Wesley Stanley, Company D seized the two Confederate cannon remaining after the explosion and turned them on their assailants to the south **(3)**. Other groups of men began to dig in. Armed with Model 1860 Spencer repeating rifles, Company K, 57th Massachusetts, commanded by Captain Benjamin A. Spear, also harassed the enemy artillery in their front **(4)**.

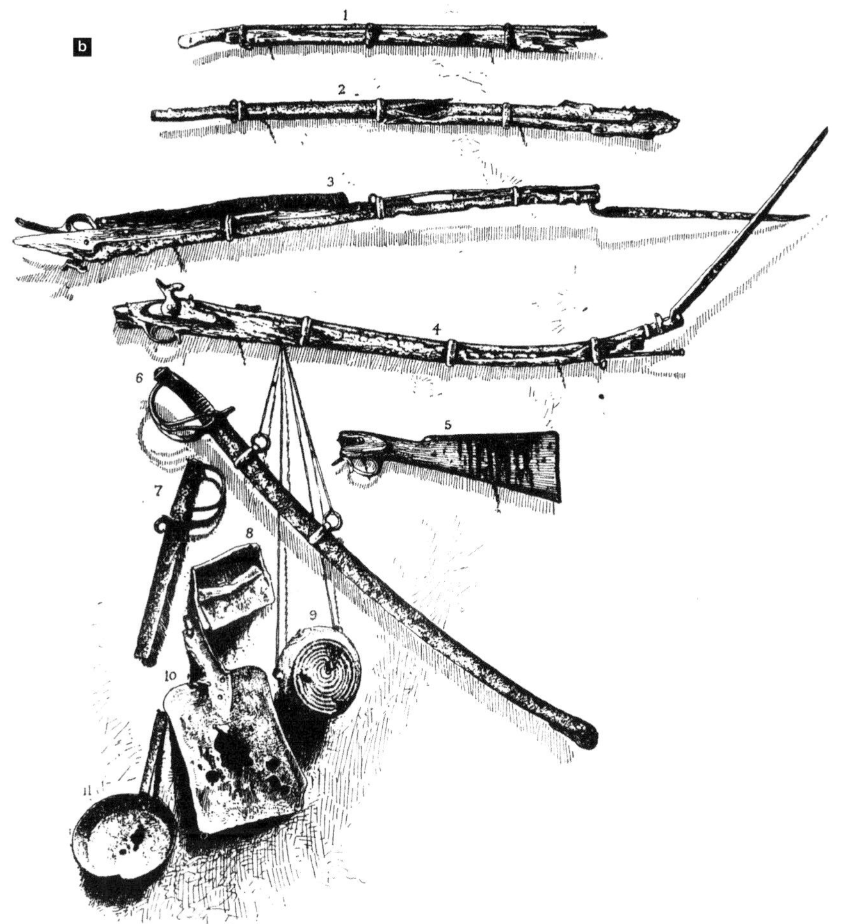

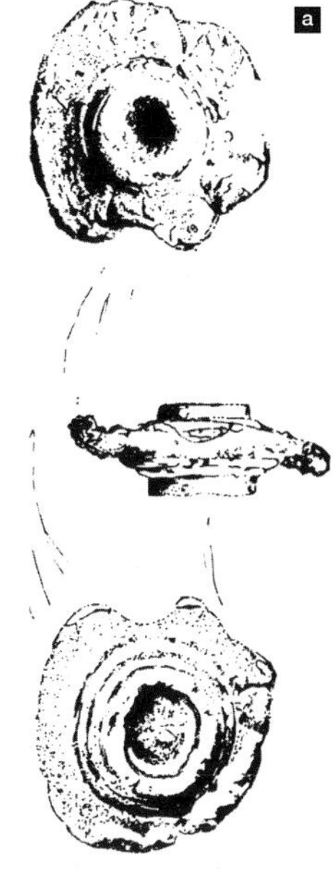

Established in 1865 by local resident William H. Griffith, whose house on the Jerusalem Plank Road was destroyed, the first museum dedicated to the Petersburg campaign contained some remarkable relics that illustrated the ferocious nature of the fighting in and around the Crater. **(a)** Front and rear view of two musket balls which met point to point. **(b) 1.** Musket barrel with a bullet hole at the muzzle. **2.** Musket burst by two bullets meeting in the barrel, a bullet having entered the muzzle as the gun was discharged. **3.** Musket struck by six bullets, one embedding itself in the barrel near the bayonet. **4.** Musket bent after having been cocked and capped. **5.** Musket stock covered with blood, found in a bombproof. **6.** Sword found in a bombproof. **7.** Broken sword. **8.** Lining of cartridge box. **9.** Canteen perforated by bullets. **10.** Shovel having bullet holes, found on the Union picket line in front of the Crater. **11.** Frying pan having bullet holes; taken out of the Crater. (*Battles & Leaders*)

two miles south of the crater, Mahone responded promptly at about 6 a.m. Choosing a circuitous route following ravines that concealed them as much as possible from observation by Union signal towers, he marched David Weisiger's Virginia brigade, and Wright's Georgia brigade, under Colonel Matthew R. Hall, toward the fighting. Reaching a ravine close by the Crater, Weisiger's brigade was ordered to lay down ready for the assault with the 6th, 16th, 61st, 41st and 12th Virginia posted from right to left. Hall's Georgians took up a similar position to the north.

As they waited for all units to arrive in position, Mahone and Weisiger observed that the Union forces occupying the rim of the Crater to their front were preparing to advance. Indeed, Lieutenant Colonel John A. Bross, 29th USCT, raised himself up and, waving the regimental colours, urged his men on yelling, "Forward, my brave boys!" At the same time Major William H. Etheredge, commanding the 41st Virginia, thought he heard the order, "Fix bayonets and no quarter" being passed along the Union line. Inevitably, Bross was cut down before the remnants of his regiment could scramble out of the Crater. However, the threat of this attack prompted the Virginians, followed by the 17th, 26th and 61st North Carolina who had formed up in their rear, to rise up and charge, yelling "no quarter" as they went in with the bayonet.

Fleeing in the face of such force, the African-Americans piled back into the crater and the trenches to its north. Captain Clark, 115th New York, recalled,

On request of General Butler, a truce was organized to bury the dead for four hours, from 5 a.m., on August 1, 1864. The report accompanying this *Frank Leslie's* engraving stated, "The bodies, after lying in a midsummer sun for two days, were terribly altered; swarms of flies gathered around these remains of the gallant fellows that fell. The rebel works swarmed with men, and in front was a line of guards. In the intervening space, between this and our line, the men were busily at work, committing to earth the remains of their comrades. Near the guards our officers met rebel officers at the flag." (Author's collection)

"The mass of the Union army are swept back like a breath of air, and are cut up badly on the backward track." Finding little sanctuary, both black and white Union troops now became so packed that they found it impossible to lift their arms or weapons to defend themselves.

Confederate Major Etheredge recorded, "we pushed to the front, and reaching the ditch, in we went with empty muskets, depending on the bayonet and breech of the gun, and a regular hand to hand encounter took place. The scene that follows beggars description: our men would drive the bayonet into one man, pull it out, turn and butt and knock the brains out of another, and so on until the ditch ran with blood of the dead and dying. So great was the slaughter that Lieutenant Colonel William H. Seward, of the Sixty-first regiment, in command, and myself ... had to make a detail [of men] to pile up the dead on the side of the ditch to make room so we could reinforce to the right or left, as occasion might require."

The Georgia brigade under Hall did not fare so well. Ordered to maneuver from their position north of the crater in order to attack the Union forces occupying that part of the salient not damaged by the mine explosion, they encountered stiff resistance from the remains of the First Brigade, Third Division, under Brigadier General John F. Hartranft, supported by the two captured Confederate cannon manned by Sergeant Stanley's New Yorkers. Other Union artillery added to the Northern firepower, which completely overwhelmed the Georgians and drove them back in utter confusion.

Nonetheless, by 9.a.m. Burnside realized the whole Union attack was a failure. Besides the carnage taking place in the Crater, supporting troops in the captured trenches to its north, including the 97th Pennsylvania, were running out of ammunition and were ordered to withdraw as best they could. Meanwhile, Mahone made preparations to wipe out the last Union resistance in the Crater by ordering the brigade of Georgians under Brigadier General John C.C. Sanders to attack. Appearing before these troops prior to the assault, Mahone advised them that General Lee himself would be watching their progress from the Gee House near the Jerusalem Plank Road. With fatal results, he added that African-American troops were in the Crater and that they should be given "no quarter." Officers were informed that the attack would take place at 2 p.m., and that two guns would be fired as a signal to charge.

Confederate artillery drew fire from the Union guns as much as possible, and then fell silent minutes before the attack began. On the sound of the signal guns, Sander's brigade rose up and advanced with shouldered arms. Captain John C. Featherston, Company F, 9th Alabama, recalled, "When we came within range we saw the flash of the sunlight on the enemy's guns as they were levelled above the walls of the wrecked fort. Then came a stream of fire and the awful roar of battle. This volley seemed to awaken the demons of hell, and appeared to be the signal for everybody within range of the fort to commence firing. We raised a yell and made a dash in order to get under the walls of the fort before their artillery could open upon us, but in this we were unsuccessful. The air seemed literally filled with missiles."

At the moment the Alabamians began their charge, the Union commanders in the Crater and nearby trenches received orders to retreat, and had begun passing the order along the line as best they could. Hence, the totally battle-shocked Northern troops offered only token resistance when the Confederates closed on them. Reaching the edge of the Crater, many fired at pointblank range while others hurled clods of earth, wood, discharged muskets, and loose cannonballs down at the terrified Union troops. Captain Featherston observed, "There were quite a number of abandoned muskets with bayonets on them lying on the ground around the fort. Our men began pitching them over the embankment, bayonet foremost, trying to harpoon the men inside."

Finally, by about 4.40 p.m. the bloodbath became too much for all, and a Confederate officer yelled out to a Union colonel nearby, "Why in hell don't you surrender?" To which the Yankee colonel replied, "Why in hell don't you let us!" At this point the remaining Union troops began to throw down their arms, and a Rebel captain urged his men to stop the violence shouting, "Hold on there; they have surrendered." The failed assault had cost the Union army 3,798 out of 20,708 troops involved. The Confederates had an estimated 11,466 men engaged. Casualties in Johnson's division (and Colquitt's brigade) were 1,182, while losses in Mahone's division, plus the 61st North Carolina, were not recorded. However, total Confederate casualties were approximately 1,500. After a 17-day court of enquiry in September 1864, Burnside was found "answerable for the want of success" of the assault following the mine explosion at Petersburg. After giving his testimony to the court, he went on a 20-day leave. On September 1, 1864 he received a dispatch from Grant instructing him not to return and John G. Parke took command of the IX Corps. Burnside finally resigned his commission on April 15, 1865 – two days after the surrender of Lee at Appomattox.

For sheltering in a bombproof while their brigades were in "difficulty in the crater," both generals Ledlie and Ferrero also bore the blame for the failure of the mine assault. The former officer resigned his commission on January 23, 1865 and returned to civil engineering. The latter remained in command for the duration, being breveted a major general of US volunteers on December 2, 1864. In his report to Chief of Staff Major General Henry W. Halleck, Grant stated: "It was the saddest affair I have witnessed in the war. Such opportunity for carrying fortifications I have never seen, and do not expect again to have." The grandson of President John Quincy Adams and commanding the African-American 5th Massachusetts Cavalry at Petersburg, Major Charles F. Adams best summed up the disastrous battle of the Crater as follows: "It was agreed that the thing was a perfect success, except that it did not succeed."

THE LONG SIEGE, AUGUST 1864 TO APRIL 1865

Grant could take little comfort from events between June 24 and July 30, 1864. Two hammer blows against Petersburg had failed. Moreover, two important railroads still connected the city with the south. On the other hand, he had accomplished an important objective. By committing the weakened but still potent Army of Northern Virginia to a defensive position in the area around the Confederate capital, he was immobilizing the South's most powerful fighting force. Furthermore, the Union failure to break through at the Crater determined the future direction of his campaign, and he determined to concentrate as much energy as possible on extending his siege lines around Petersburg.

However, other theaters of the war still clambered for attention. General Philip Sheridan had just launched his Shenandoah Valley campaign against the forces of Jubal Early and, on August 14, Grant ordered another expedition to Deep Bottom in order to prevent Lee from sending more troops to reinforce Confederate troops there. The four days of fighting that ensued proved no more conclusive than the first Deep Bottom operation of July 27–29. But once again Lee had reacted by transferring troops from Petersburg to strengthen the Richmond defenses. As a result, Grant believed that an opportunity now existed to seize and destroy the remainder of the Weldon Railroad three miles below Petersburg.

WELDON RAILROAD (GLOBE TAVERN & REAMS' STATION), AUGUST 18–21, 1864

During the early hours of August 18, Grant ordered the V Corps, commanded by Major General G.K. Warren, to carry out an attack on the railroad. Approaching via a detour to the rear on a long, wet, muddy march, Griffin's First Division of Warren's corps struck the Weldon Railroad near Globe (or Yellow) Tavern and met little opposition except from a small brigade of North Carolina cavalry under Brigadier General James Dearing.

Griffin's troops began tearing up the railroad, burning the ties, twisting the rails, leveling embankments, destroying bridges and culverts, and demolishing everything that could be of any service to the enemy in facilitating the repair of the road, should it fall back into Confederate hands. Meanwhile, Ayres' Second Division advanced up the track towards Petersburg. After progressing about three-quarters of a mile, they encountered the enemy drawn up in line of battle, supported by artillery, and a sharp fight ensued. Crawford's Third Division was next ordered up on the right of Ayres' position to outflank the Confederates. However, before this was accomplished the enemy advanced against Ayres'

General G.K. Warren used an old colonial inn called Globe Tavern as his headquarters during the first battle for the Weldon Railroad on August 18–20, 1864. (*Battles & Leaders*)

New Yorkers and Marylanders and forced his lines back by threatening to flank them. Deployed as skirmishers, the 4th Maryland Infantry reported in its after-battle report, "Engaged the enemy but was compelled to fall back, which it did in good order and reformed in rear of line of battle." Rallying his troops behind hastily thrown up breastworks, Ayres contested the ground firmly and finally drove the enemy back. According to Warren's report of this action, "the 15th New York Heavy Artillery, serving as infantry, acted very handsomely, and Lieutenant-Colonel Wiedrich, commanding, was wounded." The Union V Corps sustained 60 killed 440 wounded and 381 men missing in this action. Confederate casualties were heavy but unrecorded.

On the afternoon of the next day, four brigades of General A.P. Hill's Third Corps struck Warren's infantry. Two of these brigades managed to slip in behind that part of the Union skirmish line composed of the 190th and 191st Pennsylvania, of Crawford's division, by taking advantage of the concealment offered by the heavy growth of trees. They inflicted serious losses and captured 2,700 prisoners. By nightfall Warren had been forced back a half-mile nearer his new headquarters at Globe Tavern.

After comparative inactivity on August 20, Hill again threw his infantry at Warren's corps, which now occupied freshly dug trenches and rifle pits near Globe Tavern. According to a report in the Richmond *Daily Dispatch* the next day, "The [Confederate] column attacking in front drove the enemy back some half a mile, taking his line of breastworks and over three hundred prisoners. Here, however, they halted, owing to the strength of the enemy's next line of works, which was literally lined with artillery ... For a while our brave boys press boldly forward, but in an evil moment a brigade of ours give back, and despite the efforts of their gallant commander, refuse to rally. The contagion spreads; other troops give away, and soon the whole mass comes rushing back pell-mell, exposed to as murderous a fire in retreat as that to which they were subjected whilst advancing. Hagood's (S.C.) brigade, however, nothing daunted, actually press on amid that heavy fire of shot and shell, and reach the enemy's works. When General H. reached the works he found that one of his colonels had surrendered his regiment, of his brigade, without consulting him. At once repudiating the act of his subordinate, he ordered the men to fire and then to save themselves, his supports on the right and left having both long since fallen back. General H. himself escaped, though two horses were killed under him whilst retreating."

Although General Lee arrived with reinforcements later that afternoon, even this did not turn the tide of battle. By the end of the day Lee realized that the upper portion of the Weldon Railroad had been lost and that any attempt to regain it would be a needless sacrifice of manpower. In a dispatch to the Confederate President Jefferson Davis on August 22, he explained the seriousness of the loss of the railroad: "Our supply of corn is exhausted today, and I am informed that the small reserve in Richmond is consumed." The next day, a correspondent of the Richmond *Dispatch* stated, "To-day, for the first time in the history of the campaign of the Army of Northern Virginia, the Confederate arms have suffered a check and repulse."

For a while the Confederate government was still able to use the Weldon Railroad as far as Stony Creek Station, 20 miles south of Petersburg. At that point supplies were transferred to wagons and hauled on a 30-mile route northwest on the Flat Foot Road to Dinwiddie Court House, up the Boydton Plank Road to Petersburg, and thence on to Richmond. Construction of a branch railroad from Stony Creek Station to the Southside Railroad was also begun. Until the latter was completed, the beleaguered Confederate cities had only two direct rail communications with the south – the Richmond and Danville Railroad from Richmond and the Southside Railroad out of Petersburg, which still brought valuable supplies in from Georgia.

REAMS' STATION, AUGUST 25, 1864

Operating on the extreme right of the lines north of the James near Deep Bottom since late July, Hancock's II Corps was brought back across the river from August 18 to 20. Three days later, its 1st Division commanded by General Nelson Miles, in the absence of the ailing Francis Barlow, was ordered west toward the Weldon Railroad where they became detached from the main siege line. There they assisted in the destruction of the railroad, having occupied some poorly constructed fieldworks southeast of Reams' Station thrown up by elements of the VI Corps when sent out to meet the cavalry of Wilson and Kautz in June 1864. Semicircular in shape, they were dissected in four places by gaps left for the railroad track and road. The shortcomings of these works were to have dire consequences during the next few days.

In response to the continued destruction of one of their few remaining supply lines, A.P. Hill's Third Army Corps and Wade Hampton's cavalry were ordered to advance out of the Petersburg defenses toward Reams' Station. By 2 p.m. on August 25 Hill had launched an assault on the faulty Union breastworks and rifle pits, but this attack petered out because Hampton failed to commit his cavalry in support. Having lost the element of surprise, Hill determined that a full-scale frontal assault was needed in order to prevent the further destruction of the railroad. By 5 p.m. the Confederates were ready to launch their main assault, which began with a heavy artillery barrage, some of which demoralized Gibbon's south-facing 2nd Division by landing in its rear.

Faced with a fierce Confederate advance, elements of Miles' division, many of which were inexperienced recruits and substitutes from New York, gave way in confusion. According to an anonymous eyewitness account published in *Frank Leslie's Illustrated Newspaper* on September 19, 1864, "They approached our lines, gained the outside of our entrenchments, and at some points a hand to hand conflict ensued over the top of the breastworks, our men beating back the rebels with their bayonets, as they attempted to climb over. But soon it was found that our line was broken near the centre, and the gap

In this *Frank Leslie's* engraving based on the work of their "Special Artist" J.E. Becker, elements of Warren's corps are shown repelling the last Confederate attempt to regain control of the Weldon Railroad during the battle of Reams' Station on August 21, 1864. (Author's collection)

once made rapidly grew wider, until nearly the entire line was swept back, leaving our breastworks and artillery in the hands of the enemy, from the left of the 1st division to a point considerably to the right of the centre."

The First Brigade, 2nd Division, under Lieutenant Colonel Horace P. Rugg, was immediately ordered to fill the gap but, according to Hancock's report, these troops "could neither be made to go forward nor fire." According to Rugg, "The reserves could do nothing, as the First Division, apparently panic-stricken, were passing to the rear over our men, which made it impossible for them to fire on the enemy, and shortly after the panic spread to them, and they also left the field, except a majority of the Twentieth Massachusetts and Thirty-sixth Wisconsin Regiments, which being on the left of the line, and at the point where the enemy first crossed our works, were compelled to surrender."

With the north-facing Union line completely overrun, the remainder of Gibbon's division was exposed to attack from the rear, and was ordered to occupy the reverse side of their breastworks. With matters in a critical condition, Miles managed to rally a small force of the 61st New York, which formed at right angles to the captured Union line, re-took the guns of the 12th New York Artillery and much of breastworks. With General Miles in command, about 200 men were ordered across the railroad in an attempt to attack the Confederates in the rear, but were too few in number to succeed. According to his chief of staff, Lieutenant Colonel Charles Hale Morgan, Hancock observed the failure of this action from his headquarters, and declared, "Colonel, I do not care to die, but I pray to God I may never leave this field!"

In the midst of the chaos and confusion, Irishman Patrick Ginley, a private in Company C, 1st New York Light Artillery, had been left alone between the opposing lines. Creeping back into the works, he put three charges of canister in one of the stranded guns and fired the piece directly into a body of approaching enemy. He then rejoined the Union forces being rallied for a counterattack, and carried the colors of his command as they recaptured the works and guns. Ginley subsequently received the Medal of Honor for bravery at Reams' Station.

Meanwhile, the dismounted cavalry of Hampton's command launched an assault from west of the railroad and began to drive Gibbon's division from

OPPOSITE PAGE
The original Confederate defense works built around Petersburg between 1862 and 1864 were known as the "Dimmock Line," named for engineer Charles H. Dimmock. These stretched about ten miles around the southern approaches to the city. The 55 artillery batteries were consecutively numbered from east to west, and were linked together with rifle pits and trenches. Following the Union attacks of June 18–20, 1864 the Confederates withdrew to a secondary line of works about 1.5 miles closer to the eastern side of Petersburg. Grant ordered siege operations to begin, and Union siege lines were slowly established from east to west as one by one the main road and rail routes into the city were seized during a series of hard-fought battles.

their trenches. According to Hancock, the attack was "feeble compared with that of the enemy's infantry, and the enemy, elated at their success at this point, were pressing on with loud cheers." The Union cavalry under General David Gregg subjected the Confederates to a flanking fire, but were also forced to withdraw after Gibbon's retreating infantry. With much of his corps in complete disarray and dusk approaching, Hancock had little choice but to order its withdrawal, which was conducted in an orderly fashion with Miles' division covering the rear.

In total, the Confederates captured 9 guns, 12 regimental colors and about 2,000 prisoners at Reams' Station. The number of Union prisoners marched into the Petersburg lines was so large that the Confederate high command initially mistook them for their own troops in retreat. In his after battle report, Hancock stated: "Had my troops behaved as well as heretofore, I would have been able to defeat the enemy on this occasion ... I attribute the bad conduct of some of my troops to their great fatigue, owing to the heavy labor exacted of them and to their enormous losses during the campaign, especially in officers." Although he would have some measure of success at Hatcher's Run in October 1864, Hancock never quite recovered from Reams' Station and relinquished command of the II Corps by Thanksgiving of that year. The Confederate victory at Reams' Station meant Lee, though unable to force the Union off the Weldon Railroad completely, had minimized further damage to the railroad and had kept most of this supply line farther south intact.

HAMPTON'S "BEEFSTEAK" RAID, SEPTEMBER 14–17, 1864

As the siege of Petersburg took hold, fresh food was becoming scarce by September 1864. When Confederate scouts reported that the Union army had a herd of nearly 3,000 cattle at Coggins Point, on the south bank of the James River about five miles down from City Point, the temptation was impossible for Confederate cavalryman Wade Hampton to resist. The herd was poorly guarded by about 250 men of the 1st DC Cavalry, together with a detachment of about 150 men from the 13th Pennsylvania Cavalry. This entire area of the Union rear was picketed by the single understrength cavalry division of Augustus Kautz.

Hampton set off from his encampment near Rowanty Creek on September 14 with about 4,000 mounted troops consisting of Barringer's, Chambliss' and Dearing's brigades of cavalry, and Graham's and McGregor's batteries of artillery. The day for what became known as the "Beefsteak Raid" was chosen in part because Grant was known to be in the Shenandoah Valley in conference with Phil Sheridan.

Able to penetrate the Union rear via a roundabout route, Hampton crossed the Blackwater River at the site of a destroyed bridge which was rebuilt sufficiently for his troopers to cross that night. At dawn on the 16th, the Confederate raiders attacked and drove the Union cavalry back towards the cattle, which were enclosed in a dense abatis. The 7th Virginia Cavalry then dismounted for the assault, while the other units surrounded the enclosure. The defending Union troopers cleared a path through the abatis and tried by firing their pistols to stampede the cattle in order to get them out of reach of the Confederates. But, with the help of a large number of shepherd dogs they brought with them, Hampton's cavalry managed to head off and round up the frightened cattle. A resounding success amidst the troubles that

The defenses of Petersburg

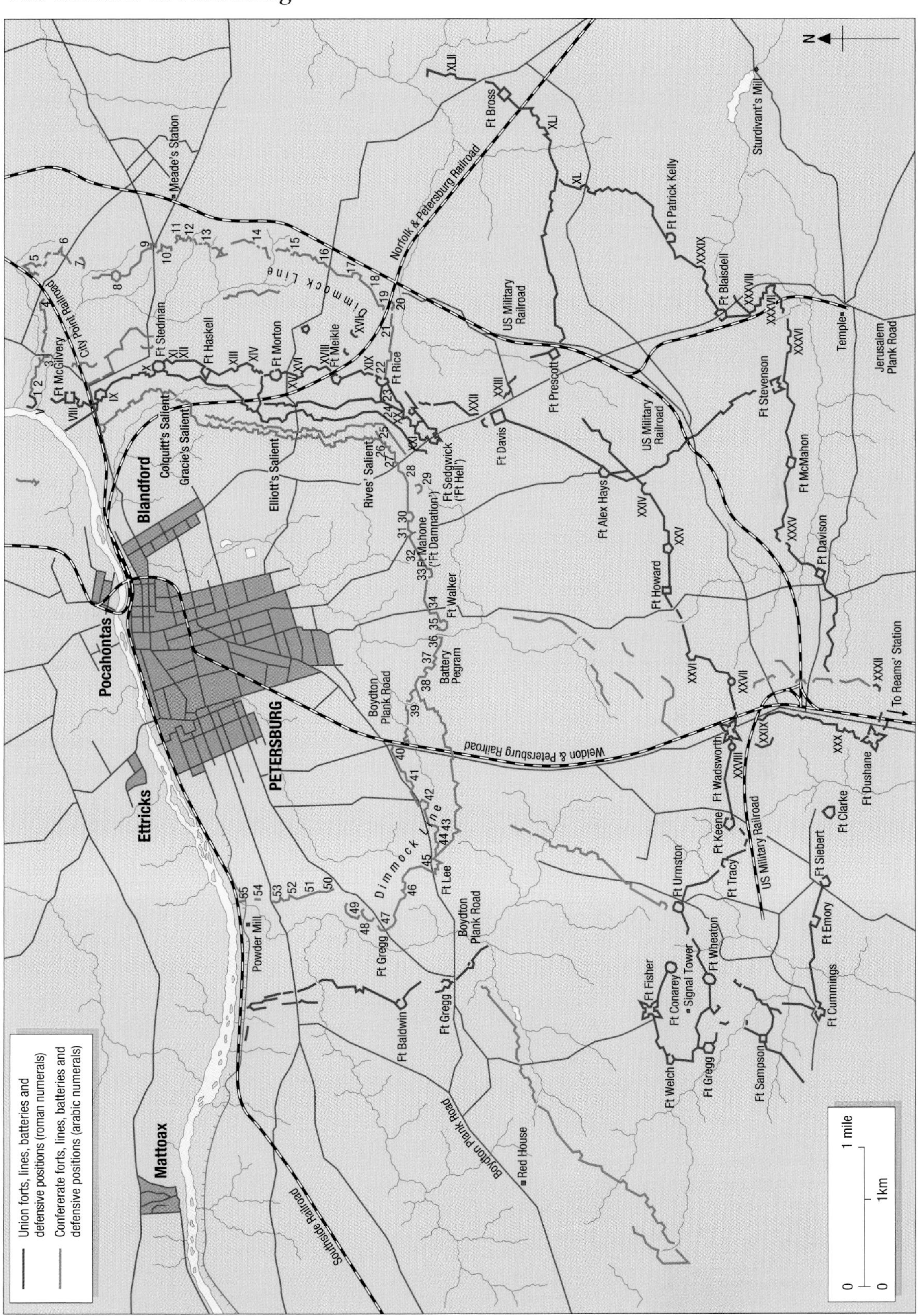

beset the Army of Virginia, the expedition rounded up and herded back toward Petersburg 2,486 head of cattle for a loss of about 50 men compared with 400 Union casualties.

After recrossing the Blackwater River, Hampton sent Rosser on ahead to hold the Jerusalem Plank Road at Ebenezer Church. Scouting northward up the road, Rosser detected a Union force of 2,100 troopers under Brigadier General Henry Davies, Jr approaching. With reinforcements, Rosser held off the Union cavalry until after dark as the cattle crossed two miles behind them. As Davies' troopers fell back, Hampton left four squadrons on picket at the church and moved the rest of his command to their former encampment on Rowanty Creek and rested for the night. The "Beefsteak Raid" encountered no further interference from Union forces and the raiders rode into the Confederate lines around Petersburg the next day.

PEEBLES' FARM (JONES' FARM), SEPTEMBER 30 TO OCTOBER 2, 1864

Once again employing the strategy of attacking the Richmond defenses in order to draw Confederate forces north of the James, and then thrusting westward around Petersburg, Grant initiated another offensive toward the end of September 1864. While the Army of the James under Butler attacked New Market Heights and Fort Harrison near Richmond on September 29 and 30, the Union commander-in-chief assigned two divisions of the IX Corps under General John G. Parke, two divisions of the V Corps under General G.K. Warren, and Gregg's cavalry division, to extend his left flank yet farther west in order to cut the remaining Confederate lines of communication, including the Boydton Plank Road and the South Side Railroad, southwest of Petersburg.

On September 30 this Union force struck out via Poplar Spring Church to reach the Squirrel Level Road by 1 p.m. and attacked the lightly manned trenches near William Peebles' Farm. They captured an incomplete earthwork or redoubt called Fort McRae and an adjacent section of breastworks, and

From an original sketch by C.H. Chapin, this *Harper's Weekly* engraving shows the first attack made by Union forces on the Confederate redoubt near Peebles' Farm, about three miles from the Weldon Railroad, on September 30, 1864. Note the V Corps divisional flag carried by the advancing troops. (Author's collection)

During the Union attack on a battery near Peebles' Farm on September 30, 1864, Lieutenant Colonel Norval E. Welch, commanding the 16th Michigan Infantry, leapt over the breastwork with sword in hand and charged at the Confederate gunners. Although he was killed shortly afterward, his men would "never forget that leap," according to the caption accompanying this *Harper's Weekly* engraving. (Author's collection)

forced the Confederates back toward the Boydton Plank Road with the loss of several pieces of artillery and 80 killed, wounded and captured. Due to clogged and narrow roads and overcaution, General Parke was not in a position to follow up this success by advancing toward the Boydton Plank Road until about 5 p.m. Meanwhile, A.P. Hill used this delay to bring up reinforcements from Petersburg. Before Parke could coordinate his assault, the Confederates counterattacked and drove the Union forces back toward Pegram's Farm, where they rallied around the 7th Rhode Island. Just before darkness fell, the Confederates attempted to continue their attack, but were unsuccessful and the fighting ended for that day. Confederate losses totaled 162 killed, wounded or missing. Amongst the dead was Colonel Edwin F. Bookter, commanding the 12th South Carolina Volunteers, McGowan's Brigade, Wilcox's Division, Third Army Corps.

Early on the morning of October 1, the Confederates attacked again at Pegram's Farm to divert attention from an attack by Heth's command along the Squirrel Level Road. Attempting to hit the troops of Warren's Corps in the rear, he was quickly repulsed. Reinforced by the Third Division, II Corps, commanded by Major General Gershom Mott, Union forces resumed their advance on October 2, recapturing Fort MacRae, which was again lightly defended, and extending their left flank to the vicinity of Peebles' and Pegram's farms. Meanwhile, Gregg's cavalry was attacked as they moved along the Vaughan Road on the Union left, but they also managed to hold the enemy at bay. With these limited successes, Meade suspended the offensive, and a new line was entrenched from the Union works on Weldon Railroad to Pegram's Farm.

BOYDTON PLANK ROAD (BURGESS' MILL OR HATCHER'S RUN), OCTOBER 27–28, 1864

By late October 1864, Grant was intent on finally cutting the last supply lines to Petersburg. This consisted of the Boydton Plank Road, which, since the break-up of part of the Weldon Railroad in late August, had carried supply wagons to Petersburg, and the South Side Railroad. Hence he launched another two-pronged Petersburg–Richmond offensive on the 27th of that month. While the Army of the James demonstrated once more against the Confederate capital, the II, V, and IX corps, plus Gregg's cavalry division,

Throughout the summer and fall of 1864, Grant's forces continued to extend his siege lines westward around Petersburg. The accompanying caption for this *Harper's Weekly* engraving stated, "The scene given in the sketch relates especially to General Warren's front. The work of fortifying goes on at night, to avoid exposure to the enemy's fire." (Author's collection)

numbering more than 30,000 men, probed yet farther west and northwest around Petersburg. As planned, the V and IX were to attack the Confederate fortifications while the II Corps cut the supply routes.

A combination of bad weather, poor terrain, and inadequate maps caused the operation to unfold too slowly. The rain fell in torrents making it impossible for Union forces to move a wheeled vehicle, except where corduroy roads were laid in their path. Moving southwest on the Vaughan Road and then northwest on the road past Dabney's Steam Saw Mill, they drove back the Confederate cavalry pickets and forged on until they struck the Boydton Plank Road. At that point, Hancock's II Corps found themselves a mile south of Burgess' Mill on Hatcher's Run. Warren's V Corps followed Hancock's route as far as the Vaughan Road Bridge farther along Hatcher's Run. Crawford's Third Division of Warren's Corps then advanced overland with its right flank on Hatcher's Run while Griffin's First Division moved in the same direction on the other side of the stream. When in place, Crawford and Griffin were to the right of Hancock's position south of Burgess' Mill. Thus, the II Corps had outflanked the Confederate right while Crawford and Griffin faced the Confederate earthworks near their southern terminus. However, a gap separated Hancock's right from the left wing of Crawford's troops.

Meanwhile, the Confederates responded rapidly to this threat. Not only did Lee order the extension westward of the line held by Heth's division in an attempt to prevent the V and IX Corps from getting to the Boydton Plank Road, but he sent Mahone's division, supported by Hampton's cavalry, to hit Hancock's II Corps along Hatcher's Run where that stream crossed the Boydton Plank Road at Burgess' Mill. Moving south through wooded lands east of Burgess' Mill, Mahone slipped through the gap between Hancock's right and Crawford's left. Deployed as skirmishers, the 1st US Sharpshooters, under Captain Benjamin M. Peck, Sergeant Alonzo Woodruff and Corporal John M. Howard, were some of the first troops of the Second Brigade, Mott's Division, commanded by Brigadier General Thomas Egan, to be hit by

Mahone's flanking movement. Peck recorded, "As the enemy passed our left flank, after both first discharging their rifles and being unable to reload, Corporal Howard ran and caught one of the enemy, who seemed to be leading that part of their line. He being overpowered, and receiving a severe wound through both legs, Sergeant Woodruff went to his assistance. Clubbing his rifle, he had a desperate hand-to-hand encounter, but succeeded in getting Corporal Howard away, and both succeeded in making their escape."

About to advance across Hatcher's Run on the Boydton Plank Road bridge, Egan's troops were hit from behind and cut off. In the desperate fight that followed, the 105th Pennsylvania were struck in the flank and lost three colors, one of which was taken by Corporal Robert Hatcher, Company E, 12th Virginia. A second flag was captured by Sergeant Thomas F. Richardson, Company K, of the same regiment. A third flag was seized by a member of the 61st Virginia. According to Captain James Miller of the 105th Pennsylvania, "the enemy charged our line and were gallantly repulsed along our entire front. They then moved around our right flank, which was unprotected, formed line of battle in the field in our rear, and poured a destructive fire on our line, killing the two senior officers of the regiment (Capts. John C. Conser and C. E. Patton). Our regiment, being almost surrounded and considerably decimated by the enemy's fire, was compelled to break through their line to prevent being captured. A large number of our men were captured and disarmed, but a portion of them succeeded in escaping to our lines. Our colors were also captured by the enemy; being surrounded there was no possibility of getting them away." Changing his front with great efficiency, Egan's troops eventually managed to fight their way back toward the main body of Union forces.

However, the Confederate maneuver failed, as Hancock left part of his corps on Hatcher's Run to engage Hampton and Heth, while reversing the other part in order to advance south, striking Mahone's troops from that direction. At the same time, Kerwin's and DeTrobriand's brigades, held in reserve by Hancock on the Boydton Plank Road a mile south of Burgess' Mill, moved north, hitting Mahone from the opposite direction. Caught in a trap, Mahone had no choice but to retire rapidly.

Still determined on success, Wade Hampton ordered five brigades of his cavalry division to dismount and charge Hancock's left and rear, but their way was blocked by Gregg's cavalry with infantry support. Riding in advance of his seasoned troopers, Hampton was accompanied by his staff which included his two sons, Lieutenants Wade Hampton, Junior, and Thomas Preston Hampton, both of whom served as aides. During the charge, Preston fell with a bullet wound to the groin. Rushing to his aid, his brother Wade was shot in the back. The former died shortly after, having been accompanied to the rear by his father. The other son eventually recovered from his wound.

Overcoming his setback at Reams' Station, Hancock had showed his old self in his last large-scale battle of the Civil War. However, Union troops were forced to withdraw back to their original positions the next day with a loss of 1,902 officers and men killed, wounded or missing. Total Confederate losses were estimated at about 500. The successful Confederate defense at Burgess' Mill meant they retained control of the Boydton Plank Road for the rest of the winter. Combined with the lack of success north of the James, it amounted to yet another failure for a Union offensive. The last major battle of the siege of Petersburg in 1864, Burgess' Mill was a turning point in Union strategy. From then on, Grant would use a single-pronged approach aimed specifically at cutting the remaining supply lines and capturing Petersburg. The approach of winter brought a general halt to most active campaigning and both armies dug in for a prolonged siege. Throughout the last two months of 1864, and the first month of the New Year, there were few major efforts by either side before Petersburg, and picket duty, sniping, and patrolling became the major preoccupation.

THE WELDON RAILROAD RAID, DECEMBER 7, 1864

The one exception was a raid conducted on the Weldon Railroad in driving rain on December 7, 1864 by Warren's corps plus Mott's division of the II Corps and Gregg's cavalry. Marching south down the Jerusalem Plank Road, this column crossed the Nottoway River by means of a pontoon at Freeman's Bridge. The next day, leaving a cavalry guard at the crossing, and protected on its flanks by cavalry, it progressed east of the railroad through Sussex Court House toward Bollings Bridge. This point was covered by enemy cavalry, which was steadily driven back. Spanning 200 feet, the bridge was reached at noon and destroyed. The raiding column was now secure against any attack from Petersburg, and proceeded to the railroad south of the Nottoway River for a distance of eight miles. The track was lifted up, ties and rails together, heaped in piles and burned. Another eight miles farther south, Jarret's Depot was burned early in the morning of the 9th, and the work of destruction continued toward Bellfield Station, near the Meherrin River. During the day two more bridges, each 60 feet wide, were burned, and that night Warren had reached Bellfield Station. Twenty miles of the railroad had been completely destroyed, and no opposition had been encountered. After a reconnaissance toward Hicksford on the Meherrin was met by a strong Confederate force, Warren turned northward through icy-cold winds, and burned Sussex Court House on the way back to his own lines on December 10, 1864.

As a result of Warren's raid, the supply route via road from Stony Creek Station, on the Weldon Railroad, to the Boydton Plank Road, which had been in use since August 1864, was destroyed. The branch railroad under construction from Stony Creek Station to the Southside Railroad since the summer suffered the same fate. Lee was now entirely cut off from eastern North Carolina, and from the portion of Virginia east of the Weldon Railroad.

HATCHER'S RUN (DABNEY'S MILLS, ROWANTY CREEK, ARMSTRONG'S MILL, VAUGHAN ROAD), FEBRUARY 5–7, 1865

In early February 1865, with Virginia still in the grips of an ice-cold winter, Grant decided to continue his campaign by launching another offensive aimed at cutting off the Confederate supply wagon traffic, which was still reaching Petersburg via the Boydton Plank Road. By that time, the Union army had managed to extend its lines about three miles west of the Weldon Railroad and seven miles southwest of Petersburg. Desperate to shield the Boydton Plank Road and Southside Railroad, their last unbroken links to the south and west, the Confederates had thrown up an additional six miles of earthworks, forming a line that curved southwest to Hatcher's Run and

LEFT Union troops make a "Greek cross," the badge of the V Corps, out of the heated rails of the Weldon Railroad during the raid conducted by General Warren on December 7, 1864.

ABOVE The cross ties being burned north of Jarret's Station on the Weldon Railroad. (Author's collection)

northwest parallel to that stream, and across the Plank Road towards the Southside Railroad and Appomattox River.

On February 5 Grant ordered the Second Cavalry Division, commanded by Brigadier General J. Irvin Gregg, southwest via Reams' Station to Dinwiddie Court House on the Boydton Plank Road to destroy as many wagons as they could find, while the V Corps, and elements of the II Corps, provided support in order to keep the Confederates at bay. Warren's Corps crossed Hatcher's Run and took up a blocking position on the Vaughan Road, while two divisions of the II Corps under Major General A.A. Humphreys shifted west to near Armstrong's Mill to cover Warren's right flank by threatening the Confederate line in the vicinity of Hatcher's Run. Despite these efforts, Gregg's troopers found the Plank Road virtually deserted and captured only a handful of prisoners and a few army wagons and teams from General Bushrod Johnson's division starting out on a foraging expedition toward Weldon.

However, fearing for the safety of his remaining supply routes, Lee ordered Gordon's Second Corps and Hill's Third Corps into action. In anticipation of such a response, Grant instructed his commanders to dig in. By mid-afternoon, the divisions commanded by generals Henry Heth and Clement A. Evans were headed south toward Hatcher's Run with orders to engage the enemy. After an abortive attempt to turn the flank of Brigadier General Thomas A. Smyth's Second Division, II Corps, the Confederates fell back to their own lines.

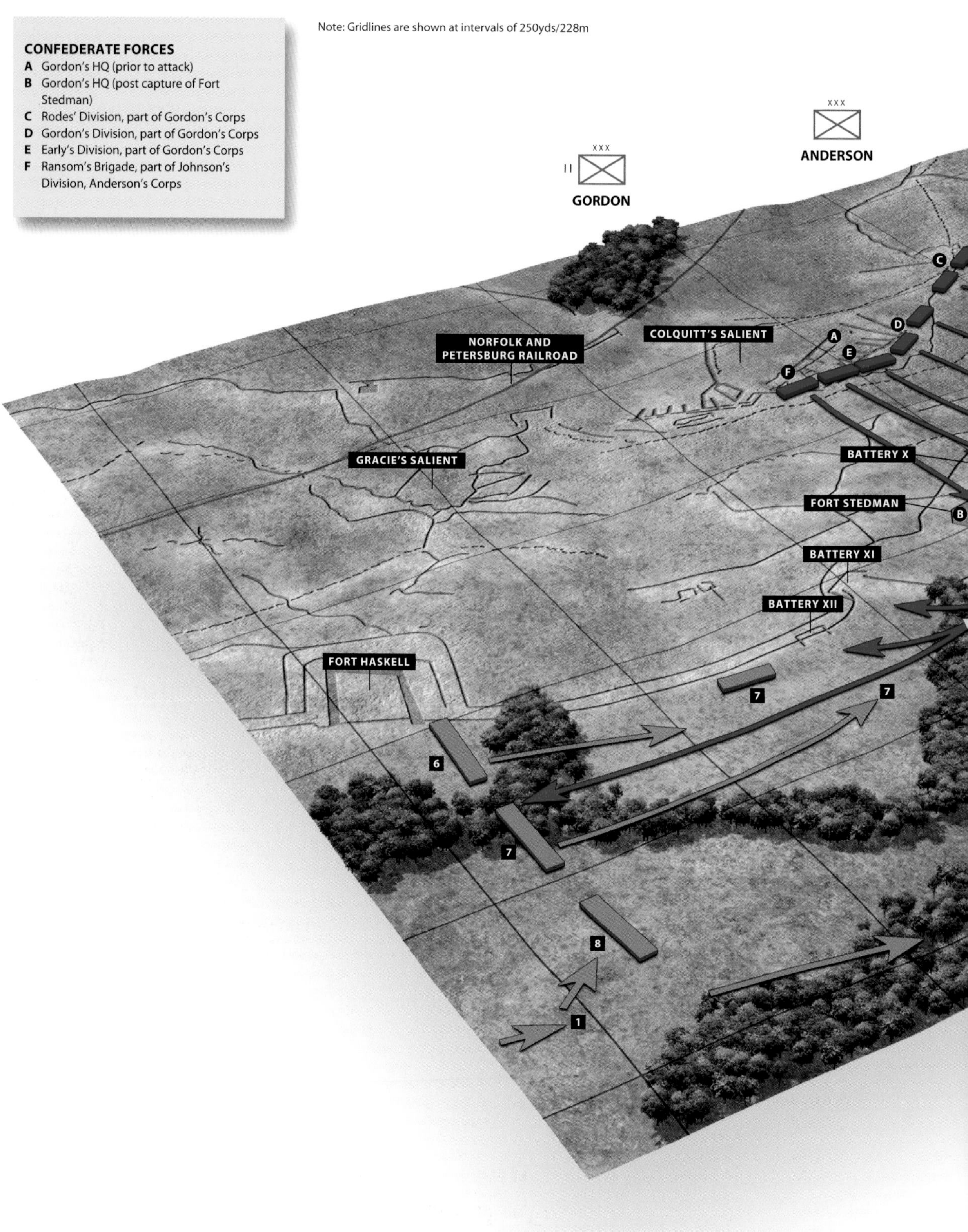
CONFEDERATE FORCES
A Gordon's HQ (prior to attack)
B Gordon's HQ (post capture of Fort Stedman)
C Rodes' Division, part of Gordon's Corps
D Gordon's Division, part of Gordon's Corps
E Early's Division, part of Gordon's Corps
F Ransom's Brigade, part of Johnson's Division, Anderson's Corps
Note: Gridlines are shown at intervals of 250yds/228m
XXX
ANDERSON
XXX
II
GORDON
NORFOLK AND PETERSBURG RAILROAD
COLQUITT'S SALIENT
GRACIE'S SALIENT
BATTERY X
FORT STEDMAN
BATTERY XI
BATTERY XII
FORT HASKELL
A
B
C
D
E
F
1
6
7
7
7
8

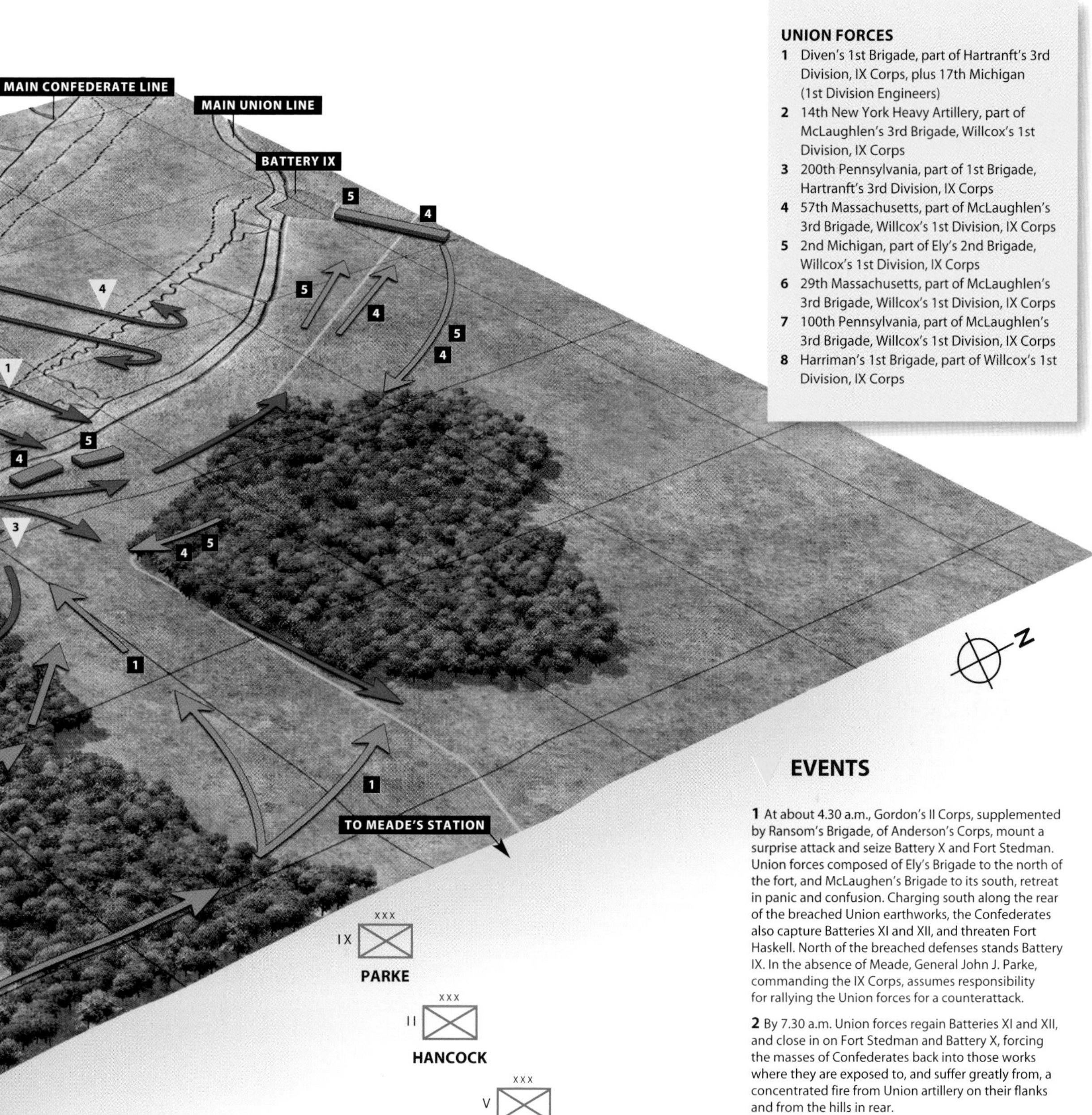

UNION FORCES

1. Diven's 1st Brigade, part of Hartranft's 3rd Division, IX Corps, plus 17th Michigan (1st Division Engineers)
2. 14th New York Heavy Artillery, part of McLaughlen's 3rd Brigade, Willcox's 1st Division, IX Corps
3. 200th Pennsylvania, part of 1st Brigade, Hartranft's 3rd Division, IX Corps
4. 57th Massachusetts, part of McLaughlen's 3rd Brigade, Willcox's 1st Division, IX Corps
5. 2nd Michigan, part of Ely's 2nd Brigade, Willcox's 1st Division, IX Corps
6. 29th Massachusetts, part of McLaughlen's 3rd Brigade, Willcox's 1st Division, IX Corps
7. 100th Pennsylvania, part of McLaughlen's 3rd Brigade, Willcox's 1st Division, IX Corps
8. Harriman's 1st Brigade, part of Willcox's 1st Division, IX Corps

EVENTS

1 At about 4.30 a.m., Gordon's II Corps, supplemented by Ransom's Brigade, of Anderson's Corps, mount a surprise attack and seize Battery X and Fort Stedman. Union forces composed of Ely's Brigade to the north of the fort, and McLaughen's Brigade to its south, retreat in panic and confusion. Charging south along the rear of the breached Union earthworks, the Confederates also capture Batteries XI and XII, and threaten Fort Haskell. North of the breached defenses stands Battery IX. In the absence of Meade, General John J. Parke, commanding the IX Corps, assumes responsibility for rallying the Union forces for a counterattack.

2 By 7.30 a.m. Union forces regain Batteries XI and XII, and close in on Fort Stedman and Battery X, forcing the masses of Confederates back into those works where they are exposed to, and suffer greatly from, a concentrated fire from Union artillery on their flanks and from the hills in rear.

3 At 7.45 a.m. Union forces retake Fort Stedman with the troops of Hartranft's Division approaching from the east, those of Ely and McLaughlen from the north and south respectively. This action is reinforced by elements of the II and V Corps.

4 The infantry and artillery crossfire on the ground between the opposing lines deters many Confederates from attempting to return to their own lines, and causes heavy losses among those who do so.

THE CONFEDERATE ASSAULT ON FORT STEDMAN, MARCH 25, 1865

On March 15 Robert E. Lee ordered corps commander John B. Gordon to formulate a plan to break out of the Union siege. Gordon chose Fort Stedman, one of the weakest points on the Union lines, as the target for attack, and massed 18,000 men for the assault.

The next day Warren initiated the action by advancing the V Corps divisions of Crawford and Ayres, screened on their left by Gregg's cavalry, northwest along Hatcher's Run. Advancing into a tangled, brush-choked terrain similar to the Wilderness of 1864, they were attacked near Dabney's Mills by the Confederates, including troops from the divisions of Finegan, Evans and Pegram. Finally, in the late afternoon the Confederate drive was stopped by Union reinforcements. Having been married only 18 days before, Brigadier General John Pegram was killed in this action while advancing at the head of his division of Virginians and North Carolinians.

By February 7, the Union forces had driven the Confederates back inside their main lines at a cost of over 2,300 casualties in their own ranks. After dark the Northern troops fell back across Hatcher's Run, but had managed to extend their trenches to the Vaughan Road crossing on that stream. The Confederates had maintained their tenuous grip on the Boydton Plank Road, but Grant had gained a good staging point for further offensive action.

THE ATTACK ON FORT STEDMAN, MARCH 25, 1865

By March 1865, the Confederate army defending Petersburg and Richmond was under increasing pressure as the supply situation worsened. Robert E. Lee wanted to go on the offensive in an attempt to join forces with the army of General Joseph E. Johnston in the Carolinas early in the year, but the roads were in a terrible condition due to spring rains. Finally, on March 15 he ordered corps commander John B. Gordon to formulate a plan to break out of the Union siege.

Gordon chose Fort Stedman as the target for attack. Opposite Colquitt's Salient and less than 300 yards from the Confederate defenses, it was one of the weakest points on the Union lines. Named for Colonel Griffin A. Stedman, Jr., 11th Connecticut Infantry, who died of wounds sustained while "reconnoitering the ground" near Gracie's Salient on August 5, 1864, Fort Stedman contained four light 12-pounder guns manned by the 19th New York Battery, and was garrisoned by 300 men of the 29th Massachusetts Infantry. A supply depot on the US Military Railroad was about a mile behind it. In a report dated April 25 of that year, Brevet General Henry L. Abbot, US Engineers, wrote that Fort Stedman was "the weakest and most ill-constructed works in the line, being not protected by abatis, or felled trees, in the rear, being masked on its right (just in rear of Battery No. 10) by a mass of bomb-proofs, rendered necessary by the terrible fire which has habitually had place in this vicinity, and being only about 200 yards distant from the enemy's main line."

By 4 a.m. on March 25, 1865 Gordon had massed 18,000 men, composed of the three divisions of his own corps, reinforced by elements of Bushrod Johnson's division of Anderson's Corps. The assault began as the first Confederate skirmishers advanced and opened up avenues through the Union defenses by quietly removing the obstacles. Using these openings, squads of picked men infiltrated forward, capturing advanced pickets and listening posts by pretending to be deserters, and opening gaps in abatis. Through these gaps came 50 axemen whose task it was to hack away sections of the fraise belt blocking the approaches to the Union fort. Close behind were three storming parties of 100 men each. This was the initial wave of a force that represented nearly half of Lee's remaining troops. The main attack came in three columns, which punched through the Union lines just north of Fort Stedman between Batteries IX and X. While the left column moved north toward Battery IX, the other two attacked Battery X and the fort.

The attack was a complete surprise as the Confederates moved quietly through the Union defenses and well before 4.30 a.m. Fort Stedman and nearby batteries had been captured with little resistance. The Confederates also overran two regimental encampments located nearby and many of the sleepy occupants were clubbed down as they staggered from their tents in alarm and panic. During the pandemonium that ensued, Sergeant Major Charles H. Pinkham, 57th Massachusetts Infantry, saved a Union flag by tearing it from the staff, and shortly after captured the flag of the 57th North Carolina Infantry. Sergeant Charles Oliver, Company M, 100th Pennsylvania, captured the flag of the 31st Georgia, and Private James T. Murphy, Company L, 1st Connecticut, helped work a recaptured gun, which laid enfilading fire on the swarming Confederate attack force. All three men subsequently received the Medal of Honor for bravery in this action.

Meanwhile, as the main Confederate force rounded up nearly 1,000 prisoners, the lead attackers became lost and confused in the labyrinth of main-line earthworks, connecting trenches, traverses and bombproofs. At the same time, the Union forces retreated and regrouped. In the absence of Meade, General John J. Parke, commanding the IX Corps, assumed responsibility for rallying the Union forces for a counterattack, and successfully managed to confine the flood of gray-clad troops to the area around Fort Stedman. Meanwhile, Union batteries in the surrounding forts delivered a heavy enfilading fire, and infantry reinforcements consisting of the First Brigade of General John F. Hartranft's Third Division, IX Corps, arrived and added their firepower as they massed for a counterattack. Watching from the Confederate lines, Lee observed Gordon's advanced parties falling back toward Fort Stedman, and quickly realized the desperate nature of the situation. By 8.00 a.m., he ordered his general to call off the attack. Hundreds of Confederates opted for surrender rather than face Union fire by withdrawing 300 yards back to their own lines. According to a report in the Petersburg *Express*, the Union artillery subjected Gordon's reeling troops to

Based on a drawing by *Harper's Weekly* artist Andrew McCallum, this engraving shows Confederate pioneers and axemen clearing Union abatis during the assault on Fort Stedman on March 25, 1865. (Author's collection)

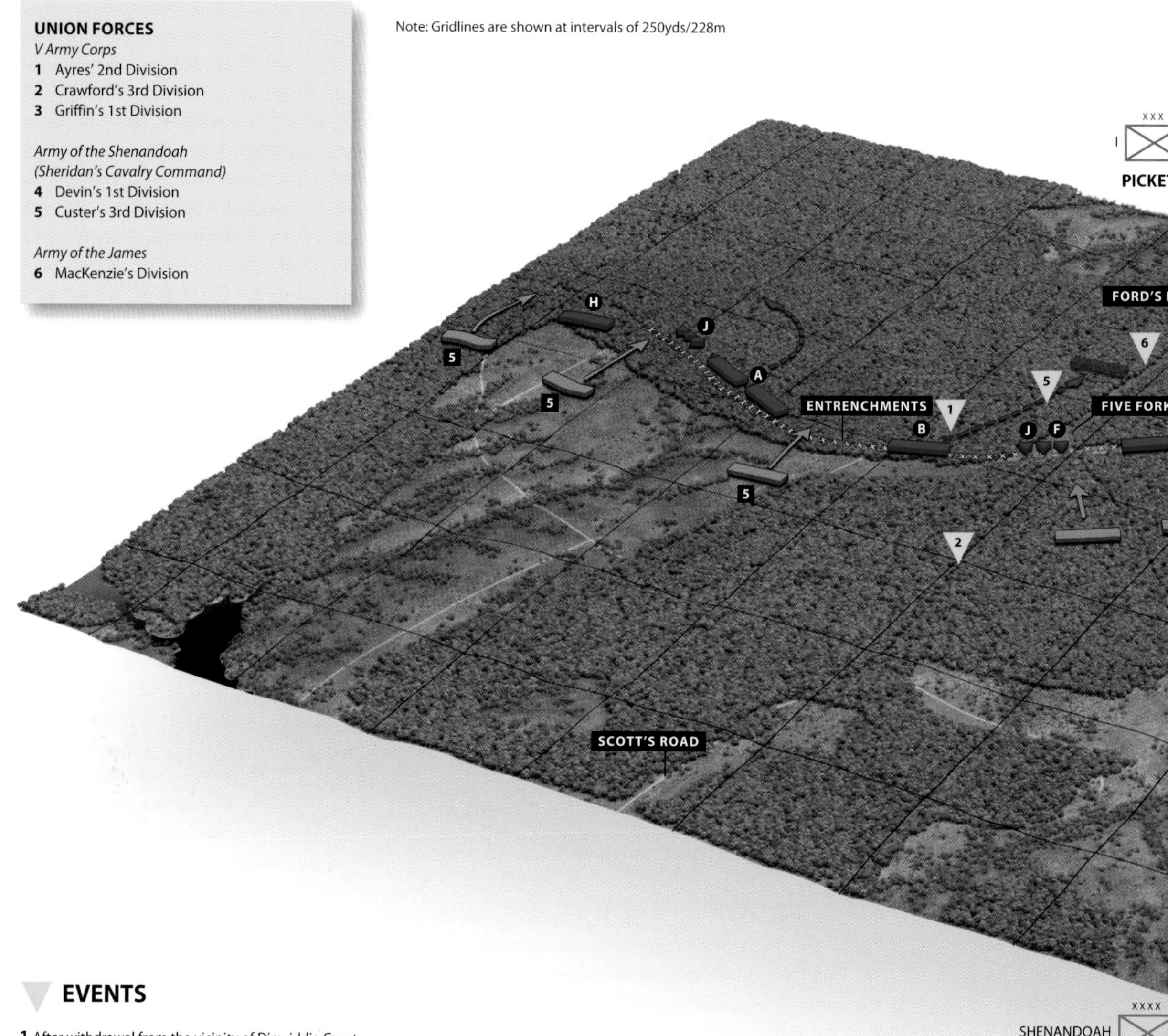

EVENTS

1 After withdrawal from the vicinity of Dinwiddie Court House during the night of March 31, 1865, Pickett mans earthworks and breastworks along the White Oak Road.

2 Midday April 1, Sheridan orders Merritt's Cavalry Division to deploy for a dismounted frontal assault to pin down the Confederate center. Meanwhile three divisions of Warren's V Corps prepare to attack Pickett's left flank.

3 Due to faulty maps and muddy roads over ground consisting of woods, fields, thickets of underbrush, swamps, ditches and streams, Warren's divisions are slow to advance and pass the right flank of Pickett's lines. After much confusion, Warren assumes immediate command of his infantry and they re-adjust in time to begin the assault at approximately 4.15 p.m.

4 By about 5.00 p.m. the full weight of Warren's infantry is overwhelming Pickett's left flank. Unable to hold back the onslaught, Confederate resistance begins to collapse.

5 Pickett, Fitzhugh Lee and Rosser race back from their shad bake at Hatcher's Run to join their forces too late to have an impact on the outcome of the battle.

6 Sheridan joins Ayres' Division and leads the charge that finally breaches Pickett's left flank. The latter folds back north towards the Falls Church Road.

7 Warren is relieved of command, and replaced by Griffin, as his corps achieves its greatest victory.

8 Fitzhugh Lee orders a cavalry charge against Custer's Division, which allows what remains of Pickett's troops to withdraw north towards Petersburg.

"THE WATERLOO OF THE CONFEDERACY" FIVE FORKS, APRIL 1, 1865

Five divisions under Major General George Pickett, combined with the cavalry of Fitzhugh Lee and Thomas Munford, attempt to hold the line along the White Oak Road as Grant's army under Phil Sheridan advance towards the Southside Railroad to finally cut off Petersburg and Richmond from supply from the south.

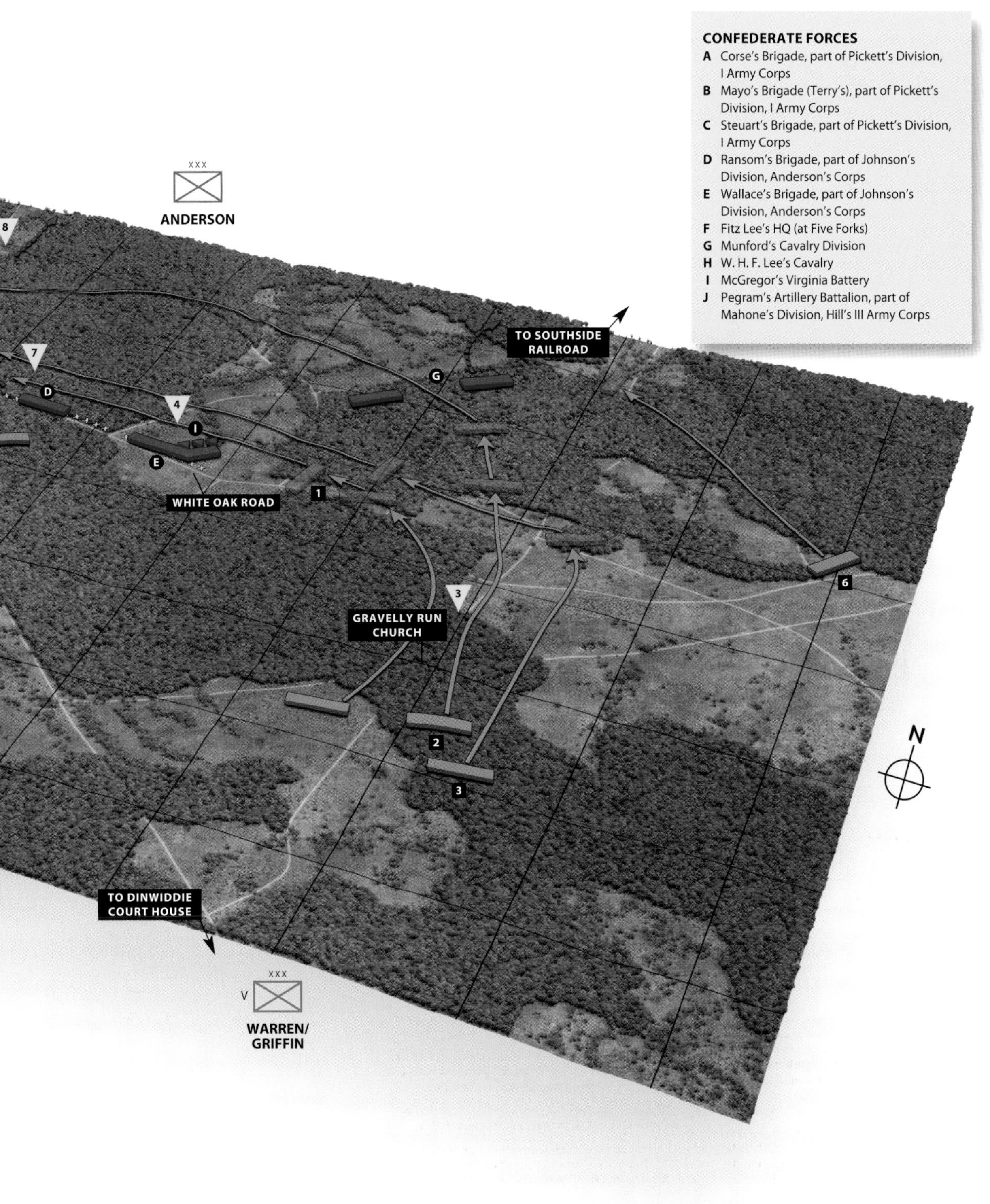

CONFEDERATE FORCES

- **A** Corse's Brigade, part of Pickett's Division, I Army Corps
- **B** Mayo's Brigade (Terry's), part of Pickett's Division, I Army Corps
- **C** Steuart's Brigade, part of Pickett's Division, I Army Corps
- **D** Ransom's Brigade, part of Johnson's Division, Anderson's Corps
- **E** Wallace's Brigade, part of Johnson's Division, Anderson's Corps
- **F** Fitz Lee's HQ (at Five Forks)
- **G** Munford's Cavalry Division
- **H** W. H. F. Lee's Cavalry
- **I** McGregor's Virginia Battery
- **J** Pegram's Artillery Battalion, part of Mahone's Division, Hill's III Army Corps

Eighteen hundred Confederate prisoners, including about 50 officers and 14 battle flags, were captured after the abortive attempt to capture Fort Stedman. This *Harper's* engraving depicts a long column of prisoners being marched into a holding area behind Union lines. (Author's collection)

"a rain of iron before which the experiences of Malvern Hill and Gettysburg are said by veterans to pale almost into insignificance. It was painfully distinct in this city, where our very dwellings were shaken to their foundations."

The attack on Fort Stedman was a disaster for Lee, as he failed to make any real impact on the Union lines. He also lost about 4,000 men while Union forces sustained 68 killed, 337 wounded, and 506 missing. In fact, the Union counterattack in conjunction with the retaking of Fort Stedman farther down the line produced greater results for Grant, as the ground gained allowed him to launch one of his breakthrough attacks on April 2, 1865.

LEWIS FARM AND WHITE OAK ROAD, MARCH 29 AND 31, 1865

In late March, cavalry commander General Philip Sheridan arrived in Petersburg having completed a successful campaign in the Shenandoah Valley. Grant instructed him to march his cavalry division west, accompanied by Warren's V Corps, in order to finally capture the Boydton Plank Road and Southside Railroad. Even if the rail route were not seized, this movement would prevent Lee from leaving Petersburg and heading to North Carolina to join Johnston. As Sheridan's troopers marched toward Dinwiddie Court House on March 29, 1865, Warren's corps turned north to take the Boydton Plank Road. The 1st Brigade, First Division, commanded by General Joshua Chamberlain, was the lead element of the V Corps as a sharp firefight ensued around the Lewis Farm. After repeated attacks and counterattacks the Confederates were driven back to their entrenchments along the White Oak Road. Chamberlain was wounded, but the Boydton Plank Road was at last in Union hands.

On March 30 Lee sent reinforcements to meet the Union effort to turn his right flank. He placed General George Pickett in charge of the Confederate effort to meet Sheridan and keep him from cutting the Southside Railroad. With three of his own brigades, and two from Johnson's division, Anderson's Corps, supported by cavalry under Fitz Lee and Thomas Munford, he prepared to meet the advance of Warren's V Corps from entrenched positions along the White Oak Road.

On March 31, part of the V Corps advanced toward the Confederate line along White Oak Road, and was repulsed by a fierce defense, which forced many of them to break and flee to the rear. Ordered to save the situation and still in pain from the wound received the day before, Joshua Chamberlain led his men into the Confederate charge that had, by that time, lost its cohesion and momentum. His troops continued the counterattack until they pushed the Confederates back into the White Oak Road breastworks and earthworks. Celebrating his greatest success since his defense of Little Round Top on July 2, 1863, Chamberlain not only saved the V Corps but cut off Pickett's force from the main Confederate lines. Having earlier that day pushed Sheridan's cavalry south toward Dinwiddie Court House, Pickett was forced to fall back to protect his left flank and the roads leading to the Southside Railroad. Attention now turned to Five Forks.

FIVE FORKS, APRIL 1, 1865

Sensing that victory was near at hand, Grant unleashed Sheridan's cavalry at Five Forks, a crossroads about 12 miles southwest of Petersburg, on April 1, 1865. His objective was the South Side Railroad, the last supply line into Petersburg. Meanwhile, aware of impending disaster and disappointed with his divisional commander's performance the day before, Lee sent a dispatch to Pickett stating, "Hold Five Forks at all hazards. Protect road to Ford's Depot and prevent Union forces from striking the Southside Railroad. Regret exceedingly your forces' withdrawal, and your inability to hold the advantage you had gained."

What followed has been dubbed the "Waterloo of the Confederacy." The troops of Pickett's division constructed a log and dirt breastwork about 1.75 miles long on the White Oak Road and posted cavalry at both flanks.

General Phil Sheridan leads the charge against the Confederate left flank at the head of Ayres' division during the battle of Five Forks on April 1, 1865. (Author's collection)

The division of cavalry under Brigadier General George A. Custer made three separate charges within an hour against the Confederate right wing at Five Forks. Repulsed on the first two occasions, they managed to break through on the third attempt. (Author's collection)

The plan of attack adopted by Sheridan was to pin down the Confederate line with the Cavalry Corps, now under Major General Wesley Merritt, while three divisions of Warren's V Corps launched an attack on Pickett's left flank. As the area in front of the Confederate position was impractical for mounted operations, Merritt's troopers were dismounted and attacked on foot.

As usual, operations did not go according to plan. Faulty maps and inaccurate intelligence led Sheridan to believe that the Confederate left flank was much farther east than it actually was. The advance of Warren's corps was slowed by muddy roads and tangled underbrush, and his troops were not ready to attack until about 3 p.m. Meanwhile, Sheridan was concerned that his troopers would run out of ammunition before the infantry was in place. Having a poor opinion of Warren, he blamed his personal leadership for the delay. As a result of the poor performance of the V corps the day before, Sheridan had also received confidential permission from Grant to relieve Warren if he saw fit.

With the Union attack about to commence, Pickett was two miles away from his battle lines enjoying a shad fish bake with generals Fitzhugh Lee and Thomas L. Rosser by the banks of Hatcher's Run. Furthermore, he had neglected to inform his men of the absence of their general officers, which left them devoid of most of their high command. With the sound of battle muffled by atmospheric conditions known as an "acoustic shadow," he was unaware of the fighting and by the time he returned to the battlefield it was too late.

Meanwhile, Warren finally advanced in a two-pronged front with Crawford's division on the right and Ayres' division on the left. Griffin's division followed up in reserve. Crawford was to strike near the end of the Confederate line at an angle, while Ayres was to hit the line head on. Due to faulty intelligence, the actual Confederate left flank was well to the west of where the Union commanders believed it was. As a result, Crawford's division missed the line completely as it moved forward, and Ayres' troops were exposed to enfilade fire from the Confederate left as they brushed past it.

The two Union divisions floundered in confusion as they attempted desperately to reorient themselves amidst the heavy thickets of underbrush.

In command of the reserve division, Charles Griffin halted his advance rather than add to the confusion. Choosing to remain in a central location, Warren sent all of his aides galloping off with orders to reorganize the attack. As this was ineffective, he rode out to take personal command. Meanwhile, accompanying Ayres' division, Sheridan personally led a charge that finally breached the left flank of Pickett's line. During this attack, 23-year-old artillery commander Lieutenant Colonel William Pegram, brother of John Pegram, was killed while directing the guns of his battalion. As the Confederates attempted to organize a new defensive line, Griffin's division advanced forward on Ayres' right and attacked. Crawford was next ordered to reorientate his division to join the fight from the north and rear of the main Confederate line, while Sheridan's cavalry swept around Pickett's right flank. After leading his men forward in one of the greatest victories achieved by the V Corps, Warren received word from Sheridan that he was relieved of command, and replaced by Major General Charles Griffin. In the last stages of the battle, Confederate cavalry under Fitzhugh Lee repulsed several charges by Union cavalry under Brigadier General George Armstrong Custer, which allowed what remained of Pickett's forces to escape.

This decisive Union victory was the breaking point for the Army of Northern Virginia, with nearly a third of Pickett's division killed, wounded or missing. The Southside Railroad, the last of the lifelines which had kept Petersburg and Richmond alive since the beginning of the campaign, was now within the grasp of Grant's army. On the morning of April 2, 1865, as Union forces launched a massive assault on the thinly defended Confederate lines, Lee informed President Jefferson Davis that Petersburg and Richmond must be evacuated.

THE FALL OF PETERSBURG

With news of success at Five Forks, Grant and Meade ordered a massive bombardment of the whole Confederate line at 10 p.m. on April 2, 1865. At 2 a.m. the following morning the bombardment stopped and 14,000 men of the three divisions of General Horatio G. Wright's VI Corps moved out of their fortifications and deployed for the attack in three large columns. The first important Union gains were made about 5.15 a.m. Attacking from the vicinity of forts Fisher and Welch, within that part of the siege line known as the "Fish Hook," the attackers crashed through the entrenchments on the right of the Confederate defenses and turned toward Petersburg. In their path stood Fort Gregg, an unfinished Confederate earthwork defending the southwestern approaches to the city (not to be confused with Union Fort Gregg). H. Clay Trumbull, the chaplain of the 10th Connecticut, described the approaches to this fort as a "deep ditch, filled breast-high with water ... An extended plain, protected by an enfilading fire, was before it." The small Confederate garrison of 214 men, consisted of the remains of the brigade of North Carolinians commanded by Brigadier General James H. Lane, plus element's of Major R. Preston Chew's Horse Artillery battalion and Walker's artillery serving as infantry. Advised by Major General Cadmus Wilcox,

Based on a sketch by Alfred Waud, troops of the IX Corps are shown in this *Harper's Weekly* engraving carrying chevaux de frise to the inward side of the fort to defend against a possible Rebel counterattack during the final capture of Fort Mahone in the early hours of April 3, 1865. (Author's collection)

The Confederate dead were photographed by T.C. Roche, a contract photographer for the US government, during the days after Fort Mahone fell. The youthfulness of many of the fallen revealed the desperate measures taken to defend the South in its final months. (Author's collection)

5TH REGT. VERMONT

FORT GREGG, APRIL 2, 1865 (PP 84–85)

With news of success at Five Forks, Grant and Meade ordered a massive bombardment of the whole Confederate line at 10 p.m. on April 1, 1865. At 2 a.m. the following morning the bombardment ceased, and 14,000 men of the three divisions of General Horatio G. Wright's VI Corps moved out of their fortifications and deployed for the attack in three large columns. The first important Union gains were made about 5.15 a.m. Attacking from the vicinity of forts Fisher and Welch, within that part of the siege line known as the "Fish Hook," the attackers crashed through the entrenchments on the right of the Confederate defenses and turned toward Petersburg. In their path stood Fort Gregg, an unfinished Confederate earthwork defending the southwestern approaches to the city (not to be confused with Union Fort Gregg).

The small Confederate garrison of 214 men consisted of the remains of the brigade of North Carolinians commanded by Brigadier General James H. Lane, plus elements of Major R. Preston Chew's Horse Artillery battalion and Walker's artillery serving as infantry. They succeeded in repulsing three successive Union attacks before overwhelming numbers of Union infantrymen finally swarmed over the breastworks of Confederate Fort Gregg.

As they did so, Private Lawrence Berry **(1)** remained at his six-pounder, and pulled the lanyard at point-blank range. According to an eyewitness, "At the climax of the fight, about a dozen Federals levelled their guns at Confederate cannoneer Private Lawrence Berry. 'Drop the lanyard or we'll shoot,' they yelled. 'Shoot and be dammed,' Berry yelled back, as he fired the cannon. He in turn fell in a blast of Union gunfire."

Confederate Corporal James W. Atkinson made his escape from the fort with the flag of the 33rd North Carolina, and as he did so Sergeant Jackson Sargent **(2)**, Company D, 5th Vermont Infantry, planted his colors inside the fort, being the first to scale the enemy breastworks. Sargent later received a Medal of Honor for his brave deed. Atkinson joined the main Confederate withdrawal and surrendered with Lee's army at Appomattox Court House a week later.

The battle for Fort Gregg lasted less than two hours, but the gallant defense bought the time Lee needed to re-establish a temporary defense line in order to conduct an orderly withdrawal from Petersburg and Richmond during the night of April 2–3, 1865. Fifty-five of the defenders were killed and 129 wounded. Federal losses of 122 killed and 592 wounded were in total more than triple the number of Confederates in the fort. As a result of this gallant stand, Lee's army was saved from total destruction and what remained of the Army of Northern Virginia evacuated Petersburg and Richmond that night.

The first Union troops to enter Petersburg on April 2, 1865, were the Michigan veterans of the 1st Brigade, 3rd Division, IX Corps, under General William G. Ely. The Union flag was raised over the Customs House in the city by men of the 2nd Michigan Infantry. (Author's collection)

"Men, the salvation of Lee's army is in your keeping," they went on to repulse three successive attacks before Union forces, on the strength of sheer numbers, breached the parapets and swarmed inside. The fighting continued hand to hand until there were only 30 defenders left to surrender.

As Corporal James W. Atkinson made his escape from the fort with the flag of the 33rd North Carolina, Sergeant Jackson Sargent, Company D, 5th Vermont Infantry, planted his colors inside the fort, being the first to scale the enemy breastworks. Sargent later received a Medal of Honor for his brave deed. Atkinson joined the main Confederate withdrawal and surrendered with Lee's army at Appomattox Court House a week later. The battle for Fort Gregg lasted less than two hours, but the gallant defense bought the time Lee needed to re-establish a temporary defense line in order to conduct an orderly withdrawal from Petersburg and Richmond during the night of April 2–3, 1865. Fifty-five of the defenders were killed and 129 were wounded. Federal losses of 122 killed and 592 wounded were in total more than triple the number of Confederates in the fort. As a result of this gallant stand, Lee's army was saved from total destruction and what remained of the Army of Northern Virginia evacuated Petersburg and Richmond that night.

Lee headed westward hoping to find supplies for his exhausted troops and to join forces with those of Joseph E. Johnston in North Carolina. President Jefferson Davis fled south with a small entourage, only to be captured on April 29, 1865. Meanwhile, on April 3, Lincoln at last fulfilled his great wish to visit Richmond. Moving about unguarded through the former Confederate capital, he was mobbed by ex-slaves who regarded him as a messiah. Instead of achieving any of his objectives, Lee found himself surrounded by Union forces. Attempting to break out, he fought his last battle at Sayler's Creek on April 6, 1865, which achieved little except the loss of a further 8,000 men. By April 9, he realized that further resistance was pointless, and stated to his generals: "There is nothing left for me to do but go and see General Grant and I would rather die a thousand deaths." Lee met Grant in the front parlor of a farmhouse owned by Abner McLean at Appomattox Court House, and surrendered the remnants of the Army of Northern Virginia. Grant was magnanimous in victory, and permitted the Confederate troops to keep their side arms, personal possessions and horses. He also issued Union army rations to the starving Southerners. Meeting his troops for one last time that day, he told them, "Boys, I have done the best I could for you. Go home now, and if you make as good citizens as you have soldiers, you will do well, and I shall always be proud of you."

THE BATTLEFIELD TODAY

The smoke of battle had hardly cleared when the curious began to visit the battlefields of the Petersburg campaign. As early as August 19, 1865, *Frank Leslie's Illustrated Newspaper* published an engraving showing tourists gathered around the Crater. Before the year was out, a Confederate veteran had opened a "retreat" near Fort Stedman, which served everything from liquor to lemonade for thirsty battlefield wanderers. Meanwhile, preservation of the Crater, plus a museum, was begun by landowner William H. Griffith, whose house along the Jerusalem Plank Road was destroyed during the siege.

The first effort to develop a battlefield park began in 1898 when the Petersburg National Battlefield Association was formed. Efforts to introduce a bill to US Congress on the part of this organization were unsuccessful at this time, probably because of the impending war with Spain. In 1923 Carter R. Bishop, another Confederate veteran, renewed the campaign to establish a battle park and finally, on July 3, 1926, President Calvin Coolidge signed the bill authorizing the establishment of Petersburg National Military Park. Initially under the jurisdiction of the War Department, by1936 the battlefield site had been officially transferred to the National Park Service.

In 1956 the Park Service began a 10-year conservation and development project known as the "Mission 66 Development Program." In 1961 the battlefield was designated a National Historic Landmark and on August 24, 1962 Congress authorized and funded the acquisition of the land, and changed the name of the park to the Petersburg National Battlefield.

In 1959 the Dinwiddie County Civil War Centennial Commission endorsed the establishment of a park unit preserving the Five Forks battlefield. A study determined that about 1,200 acres would be needed to protect the site. This was finally realized after 27 years and five attempts, when in October 1989 the Richard King Mellon Foundation, assisted by the Conservation Fund, purchased 930 acres of the battlefield from the major landowner of the property.

A tour of the Petersburg National Battlefield today consists of a four-mile drive, included within which are four short, interpretative walking trails. The Visitor Center, or Tour Stop 1, contains a three-dimensional map presentation of the military operations during the Petersburg campaign. Along a short walking trail nearby are Battery 5 and about a mile of the Dimmock Line, or original Confederate earthworks captured by Union forces from June 15–18, 1864. Tour Stops 2 and 3 consist of Batteries 8 and 9 of the Dimmock line which were gallantly stormed by US Colored Troops during the same assault. A reconstruction of a sutler store and Union encampment are manned by living historians at this location during the summer months. At Tour Stop 4 is Harrison's Creek, which the Confederates held for two days after the collapse of the eastern end of the Dimmock Line. The grass-covered earthworks of Fort Stedman are found at Tour Stop 5, plus a loop trail which leads to Colquitt's Salient where originated the Confederate attack of March 25, 1865. This trail passes the Monument commemorating the bravery of the 1st Maine Heavy Artillery on June 18, 1864, when they sustained the highest regimental loss in a single battle action of the Civil War. At Tour Stop 6 are the remains of Fort Haskell, the guns of which helped Union forces retake Fort Stedman on the above date. Tour Stop 7 is located at the site of the Taylor Farm, nearby which 200 Union guns were concentrated and fired during the battle of the Crater on July 30, 1864. The remains of the Crater are at Tour Stop 8, seen via a short walking trail which passes the entrance to the Union tunnel and follows its path to the now grass-covered crater itself.

An extended driving tour of about 16 miles leads to battlefield park areas south and west of Petersburg. Although modern development has obliterated most of the trenches, some traces are still to be found at various points. This part of the tour begins with a left turn out of the Petersburg unit, which leads along Crater Road, known as the Jerusalem Plank Road during the Civil War period. The Union earthworks were generally located to the left of this road and the Confederate works were to the right. Leveled in the late 1960s, Tour Stop 9 at the southeast corner of Crater Road and Morton Avenue is the site of Fort Sedgwick, also known as "Fort Hell" because it exchanged fire continuously during the siege. Tour Stop 10 is the location of Fort Wadsworth, which was a Union fort built on the site of the battle of Weldon Railroad of August 1864. The present-day Halifax Road follows the original route of the railroad. The monument dedicated to approximately 1,500 South Carolinian volunteers who fell while serving in this area stands nearby. The site of Globe Tavern, which served as Warren's headquarters during the battle of Weldon Railroad, stands about half a mile southeast. The remains of Fort Wadsworth are now under private ownership. Poplar Grove cemetery at Tour Stop 11 contains the remains of 6,314 Confederate and Union soldiers who died in the Petersburg and Appomattox campaigns. About two-thirds of these graves are marked "unknown." The remains of another 5,000 Union soldiers who died of wounds or disease in the hospitals at City Point were buried in makeshift cemeteries nearby. These were later re-interred in the City Point National Cemetery in Hopewell. Many of the Confederate soldiers who died during the campaign and siege were buried in mass graves at Blandford Cemetery in Petersburg. Tour Stops 12 and 13 demark the sites of Union Forts Urmston and Conahey, both of which were built during October 1864 on ground which earlier witnessed the battle at Peebles' Farm. The largest earthwork on the Union siege line, the remains of Fort Fisher stand at Tour Stop 14. As the Confederate lines were about a mile north, this fort saw no fighting. Also on that section of the Union siege lines known as "The Fish Hook," the tree-covered remains of Fort Gregg stand at Tour Stop 15. Tour Stop 16 is devoted to Five Forks, a country road junction about 12 miles southwest of Petersburg, and six miles north of Dinwiddie Court House, where Sheridan finally broke through Pickett's division on April 1, 1865.

About three miles northeast of Petersburg, the City Point unit was the site of the largest field supply base of the Civil War, and visitors today can see the renovated remains of the cabin used by Grant as his headquarters during much of the Petersburg campaign.

ORDER OF BATTLE

THE ARMY OF THE POTOMAC

Approximately 107,500 men.
Commander: Lieutenant General Ulysses S. Grant, General-in-Chief of the Armies of the United States
Major General George G. Meade

Escort
Companies B, F, & K, 5th US Cavalry
4th US Infantry

Provost Guard
Brigadier General Marsena R. Patrick
1st Indiana Cavalry (companies I and K)
1st Massachusetts Cavalry (companies C and D)
80th New York Infantry (20th Militia)
3rd Pennsylvania Cavalry (8 companies)
68th Pennsylvania Infantry
114th Pennsylvania Infantry

Engineer Brigade
Brigadier General Henry W. Benham
15th New York Engineers (5 companies)
50th New York Engineers (5 companies)
Battalion US Engineers

Guards and Orderlies
Oneida (New York) Cavalry

Artillery
Brigadier General Henry J. Hunt (chief of artillery).
Colonel Henry L. Abbot (siege artillery)
1st Connecticut Heavy Artillery (5 companies)
1st Connecticut Heavy Artillery (7 companies)
3rd Connecticut Battery

Signal Corps
Captain Benjamin F. Fisher

II ARMY CORPS
Major Generals Winfield Scott Hancock and David B. Birney

Escort
1st Vermont Cavalry (Company M)

Engineers
50th New York (1st Battalion)

First Division
Brigadier General Francis C. Barlow

First Brigade
Brigadier General Nelson A. Miles
26th Michigan
5th New Hampshire
2nd New York Heavy Artillery
61st New York
81st Pennsylvania
140th Pennsylvania
183rd Pennsylvania

Second Brigade
Colonel Patrick Kelly
28th Massachusetts (5 companies)
7th New York Heavy Artillery
63rd New York (6 companies)
69th New York (6 companies)
88th New York (5 companies)

Third Brigade
Colonel Clinton D. MacDougall
7th New York Veteran
39th New York
52nd New York
57th New York
111th New York
125th New York
126th New York (5 companies)

Fourth Brigade
Colonel James A. Beaver
4th New York Heavy Artillery
64th New York (6 companies)
66th New York
53rd Pennsylvania
116th Pennsylvania
145th Pennsylvania
148th Pennsylvania

Second Division
Major General John Gibbon
Brigadier General Thomas A. Smyth

Provost Guard
2nd Company Minnesota Sharpshooters
First Brigade
Brigadier General Byron R. Pierce
19th Maine
15th Massachusetts
19th Massachusetts
20th Massachusetts
1st Company Andrew (Massachusetts) Sharpshooters
7th Michigan
1st Minnesota (2 companies)
42nd New York
59th New York
82nd New York
184th Pennsylvania
36th Wisconsin

Second Brigade
Colonel John Fraser
152nd New York
69th Pennsylvania
72nd Pennsylvania
106th Pennsylvania

Third Brigade
Colonel Thomas A. Smyth
14th Connecticut
1st Delaware
12th New Jersey
10th New York (battalion)
108th New York
4th Ohio (battalion)
8th Ohio
7th West Virginia

Fourth Brigade
Colonel John Ramsey
8th New York Heavy Artillery
155th New York
164th New York
170th New York
182d New York

Third Division
Brigadier General Gershom Mott

First Brigade
Colonel Thomas W. Egan
20th Indiana
17th Maine
40th New York
86th New York
124th New York
99th Pennsylvania
110th Pennsylvania
141st Pennsylvania
2nd US Sharpshooters

Second Brigade
Colonel Thomas R. Tannatt
1st Massachusetts Heavy Artillery
5th Michigan
93rd New York
57th Pennsylvania
63rd Pennsylvania
105th Pennsylvania
1st US Sharpshooters (2 companies)
141st Pennsylvania

Third Brigade
Colonel Daniel Chaplin
1st Maine Heavy Artillery
16th Massachusetts
5th New Jersey
6th New Jersey
7th New Jersey (battalion)
8th New Jersey (battalion)
11th New Jersey
115th Pennsylvania

Fourth Brigade
Colonel William Brewster
11th Massachusetts (battalion)
71st New York
72nd New York
73rd New York
74th New York
120th New York
84th Pennsylvania (4 companies)

Artillery Brigade
Colonel John C. Tidball
Maine Light, 6th Battery
Massachusetts Light, 10th Battery
New Hampshire Light, 1st Battery
1st New Jersey Light, Battery B
New Jersey Light, 3rd Battery
2nd New Jersey
4th New York Heavy, Battery L
1st New York Light, Battery G
New York Light, 11th Battery
New York Light, 12th Battery
1st Pennsylvania Light, Battery F
1st Rhode Island Light, Battery A
1st Rhode Island Light, Battery B
4th US, Battery K
5th US, Batteries C and I

V ARMY CORPS
Major General Gouverneur K. Warren

Escort
1st Michigan Cavalry (detachment)

Provost Guard
5th New York (battalion)

First Division
Brigadier General Charles Griffin

First Brigade
Brigadier General Joshua L. Chamberlain
121st Pennsylvania
142nd Pennsylvania
143rd Pennsylvania
149th Pennsylvania
150th Pennsylvania
187th Pennsylvania

Second Brigade
Colonel Jacob B. Sweitzer
22nd Massachusetts
32nd Massachusetts
4th Michigan
62nd Pennsylvania
91st Pennsylvania
155th Pennsylvania
21st Pennsylvania

Third Brigade
Brigadier General Joseph J. Bartlett
20th Maine
18th Massachusetts
1st Michigan
16th Michigan
44th New York
83rd Pennsylvania (6 companies)
118th Pennsylvania

Second Division
Brigadier General Romeyn B. Ayres

First Brigade
Brigadier General Frederic Winthrop/Colonel Edgar M. Gregory
5th New York
140th New York
146th New York
4th US
10th US (3 companies)
11th US (6 companies)
12th US
14th US
17th US

Second Brigade
Colonel Nathan T. Dushane
1st Maryland
4th Maryland
7th Maryland
8th Maryland
Purnell Legion (Maryland)

Third Brigade
Colonel J. Howard Kitching
6th New York Heavy Artillery
15th New York Heavy Artillery

Third Division
Brigadier General Samuel W. Crawford

First Brigade
Colonel Peter Lyle
16th Maine
13th Massachusetts
39th Massachusetts
104th New York
90th Pennsylvania
107th Pennsylvania

Second Brigade
Colonel James L. Bates
12th Massachusetts
94th New York
97th New York
11th Pennsylvania
88th Pennsylvania

Third Brigade
Colonel James Cable
190th Pennsylvania (1st Veteran Reserves)
191st Pennsylvania (1st Veteran Reserves)

Fourth Division
Brigadier General Lysander Cutler

Provost Guard
Independent Battalion (Wisconsin)

First Brigade
Colonel Edward S. Bragg
7th Indiana
19th Indiana
24th Michigan
1st Battalion New York Sharpshooters
6th Wisconsin
7th Wisconsin

Second Brigade
Colonel J. William Hofmann
3rd Delaware
4th Delaware
76th New York
95th New York
147th New York
56th Pennsylvania
157th Pennsylvania

Artillery Brigade
Colonel Charles Wainwright
Massachusetts Light, 3rd Battery (C)
Massachusetts Light, 5th Battery (E)
Massachusetts Light, 9th Battery
1st New York, Battery B
1st New York, Battery C
1st New York, Battery C
1st New York, Battery E
1st New York, Battery H
1st New York, Battery L
1st Pennsylvania Light, Battery B
4th US, Battery B
5th US, Battery D

Pontoniers
Massachusetts Heavy Artillery (pontoniers), 13th Company

VI ARMY CORPS
Major General Horatio G. Wright

Escort
8th Pennsylvania Cavalry, Company A

Engineers
50th New York, 2nd Battalion

First Division
Brigadier General David A. Russell

First Brigade
Colonel William H. Penrose
1st Delaware Cavalry (dismounted)
4th New Jersey
10th New Jersey
15th New Jersey (1 company 3rd New Jersey attached)

Second Brigade
Brigadier General Emory Upton
2nd Connecticut Heavy Artillery
5th Maine
121st New York
95th Pennsylvania (6 companies)
96th Pennsylvania

Third Brigade
Lieutenant Colonel Gideon Clark
6th Maine
49th Pennsylvania
119th Pennsylvania
5th Wisconsin

Fourth Brigade
Colonel Joseph E. Hamblin
65th New York
67th New York
122nd New York
23rd Pennsylvania
82nd Pennsylvania

Second Division
Brigadier General Thomas H. Neill

First Brigade
Brigadier General Frank Wheaton
62nd New York
93rd Pennsylvania
98th Pennsylvania
102nd Pennsylvania
139th Pennsylvania

Second Brigade
Brigadier General Lewis A. Grant
2nd Vermont
3rd and 4th Vermont
5th Vermont
6th Vermont (6 companies)
11th Vermont (1st Heavy Artillery)

Third Brigade
Colonel Daniel D. Bidwell
7th Maine
43rd New York (5 companies)
49th New York (5 companies)
77th New York (5 companies)
61st Pennsylvania
Fourth Brigade
Colonel Oliver Edwards
7th Massachusetts
10th Massachusetts
37th Massachusetts
2nd Rhode Island (detachment)

Third Division
Brigadier General James B. Ricketts

First Brigade
Colonel Willard S. Truex
14th New Jersey
106th New York
151st New York (5 companies)
87th Pennsylvania (5 companies)
10th Vermont

Second Brigade
Colonel Benjamin F. Smith
6th Maryland
9th New York Heavy Artillery
110th Ohio
122nd Ohio
126th Ohio
67th Pennsylvania
138th Pennsylvania

Cavalry Detachment
Colonel Charles Tomkins
22nd New York (detachment)
18th Pennsylvania (detachment)

Artillery Brigade
Colonel Charles H. Tompkins
Maine Light, 4th Battery (D)
Maine Light, 5th Battery (E)
Massachusetts Light, 1st Battery (A)
1st New Jersey Light, Battery A
New York Light, 3rd Battery
1st Ohio Light, Battery H
1st Rhode Island Light, Battery C
1st Rhode Island Light, Battery E
1st Rhode Island Light, Battery G
5th US, Battery E
5th US, Battery M

IX ARMY CORPS
Major General Ambrose E. Burnside/John G. Parke

Provost Guard
8th US Infantry

First Division
Brigadier General James H. Ledlie

First Brigade
Brigadier General William F. Bartlett
21st Massachusetts
29th Massachusetts
35th Massachusetts (acting engineers)
56th Massachusetts
57th Massachusetts
59th Massachusetts
100th Pennsylvania

Second Brigade
Colonel Elisha G. Marshall
2nd Pennsylvania Provisional Heavy Artillery
14th New York Heavy Artillery
3rd Maryland (4 companies)
179th New York

Third Brigade
Brigadier General Napoleon B. McLaughlen
3rd Maryland (battalion)
29th Massachusetts
57th Massachusetts
59th Massachusetts
14th New York Heavy Artillery
100th Pennsylvania

Engineers
35th Massachusetts

Artillery
Captain John B. Eaton
Maine Light, 2nd Battery (B)
Massachusetts Light, 14th Battery
New York Light, 27th Battery

Second Division
Brigadier General Robert B. Potter

First Brigade
Colonel John I. Curtin
36th Massachusetts
58th Massachusetts
2nd New York Mounted Rifles (dismounted)
45th Pennsylvania
48th Pennsylvania
7th Rhode Island

Second Brigade
Brigadier General Simon G. Griffin
2nd Maryland
31st Maine
32nd Maine
6th New Hampshire
9th New Hampshire
11th New Hampshire
17th Vermont

Acting Engineers
51st New York

Artillery
Massachusetts Light, 11th Battery
New York Light, 19th Battery

Third Division
Brigadier General Orlando B. Willcox/Brigadier General John F. Hartranft

First Brigade
Brigadier General William G. Ely
8th Michigan
20th Michigan
27th Michigan
109th New York
13th Ohio Cavalry (dismounted)
51st Pennsylvania
37th Wisconsin
38th Wisconsin (4 companies)

Second Brigade
Colonel Benjamin C. Christ
1st Michigan Sharpshooters
2nd Michigan
24th New York Cavalry (dismounted)
46th New York
60th Ohio
50th Pennsylvania

Acting Engineers
17th Michigan

Artillery
Maine Light, 7th Battery (G)
New York Light, 34th Battery

Fourth Division
Brigadier General Edward Ferrero

First Brigade
Colonel Joshua K. Sigfried
27th US Colored Troops
30th US Colored Troops
39th US Colored Troops
43rd US Colored Troops

Second Brigade
Colonel Henry G. Thomas
19th US Colored Troops
23rd US Colored Troops
28th US Colored Troops
29th US Colored Troops
31st US Colored Troops

Artillery
Pennsylvania Light, Battery D, Captain Samuel H. Rhoads
Vermont Light, 3rd Battery

CAVALRY

Second Division
Brigadier General David McM. Gregg

First Brigade
Brigadier General Henry E. Davies, Jr
1st Massachusetts
1st New Jersey
10th New York
1st Pennsylvania

Second Brigade
Colonel J. Irvin Gregg
1st Maine
2nd Pennsylvania
4th Pennsylvania
8th Pennsylvania
13th Pennsylvania
16th Pennsylvania

Third Division
Brigadier General James H. Wilson

First Brigade
Colonel John B. McIntosh
1st Connecticut
3rd New Jersey
2nd New York
5th New York
2nd Ohio

Second Brigade
Colonel George H. Chapman
3rd Indiana
1st New Hampshire
8th New York
22nd New York
1st Vermont

Horse Artillery Brigade
Captain James M. Robertson
1st US, Batteries H and I
1st US, Battery K
2nd US, Battery A
2nd US, Batteries B and L
2nd US, Battery D
2nd US, Battery M
3rd US, Battery C
4th US, Batteries C and E

ARMY OF THE JAMES
Major General Benjamin F. Butler

X ARMY CORPS
Brigadier General Robert S. Foster

First Division
Brigadier General Alfred H. Terry

First Brigade
Colonel Joshua B. Howell
39th Illinois
62nd Ohio
67th Ohio
85th Pennsylvania

Second Brigade
Colonel Joseph R. Hawley
6th Connecticut
7th Connecticut
3rd New Hampshire
7th New Hampshire

Third Brigade
Colonel Harris M. Plaisted
10th Connecticut
11th Maine
1st Maryland Cavalry (dismounted)
24th Massachusetts
100th New York

Artillery Brigade
Captain Loomis L. Langdon
Connecticut Light, 1st Battery
New Jersey Light, 5th Battery
1st United States, Battery M

Second Division
Brigadier General Adelbert Ames

First Brigade
Colonel N. Martin Curtis
3rd New York
112th New York
117th New York
142nd New York

Second Brigade
Colonel William B. Barton
47th New York
48th New York
115th New York
76th Pennsylvania

Third Brigade
Colonel Louis Bell
13th Indiana
9th Maine
4th New Hampshire
169th New York
97th Pennsylvania

Artillery
New Jersey Light, 4th Battery
1st US, Battery D
3rd US, Battery E
4th US, Battery D

Third Division
Brigadier General Orris S. Ferry

First Brigade
Brigadier General Gilman Marston
133rd Ohio
143rd Ohio
148th Ohio
163rd Ohio
New York Light Artillery, 33rd Battery

Second Brigade
Colonel James B. Armstrong
130th Ohio
132nd Ohio
134th Ohio
138th Ohio
142nd Ohio
37th US Colored Troops (attached)

XVIII ARMY CORPS
Major General William F. "Baldy" Smith

Provost Guard
2nd New Hampshire
79th New York (1 company)

First Division
Brigadier General William T.H. Brooks

First Brigade
Colonel Edgar M. Cullen
81st New York
96th New York
98th New York
139th New York

Second Brigade
Brigadier General Hiram Burnham
8th Connecticut
10th New Hampshire
13th New Hampshire
118th New York

Third Brigade
Colonel Guy V. Henry
21st Connecticut
40th Massachusetts
92nd New York
58th Pennsylvania
188th Pennsylvania

Second Division
Brigadier General John H. Martindale

First Brigade
Brigadier General George J. Stannard
23rd Massachusetts
25th Massachusetts
27th Massachusetts
9th New Jersey
55th Pennsylvania

Second Brigade
Colonel Griffin A. Stedman, Jr
11th Connecticut
8th Maine
12th New Hampshire
148th New York
19th Wisconsin

Third Brigade
Colonel Augustus A. Gibson
5th Maryland
89th New York
2nd Pennsylvania Heavy Artillery

Third Division
Brigadier General Edward W. Hinks

Cavalry
4th Massachusetts (detachment)

First Brigade
Brigadier General Edward A. Wild
5th Massachusetts Colored Cavalry (dismounted)
1st US Colored Cavalry (dismounted)
1st US Colored Troops
10th US Colored Troops

Second Brigade
Colonel Samuel A. Duncan
2nd US Colored Cavalry (dismounted)
4th US Colored Troops

5th US Colored Troops
6th US Colored Troops
22nd US Colored Troops

Artillery Brigade
Colonel Henry S. Burton
3rd New York Light, Battery E
3rd New York Light, Battery K
3rd New York Light, Battery M
New York Light, 7th Battery
New York Light, 16th Battery
1st Rhode Island Light, Battery F
Wisconsin Light, 4th Battery
1st US, Battery B
4th US Battery L
5th US Battery A
2nd US Colored Light, Battery B

Naval Brigade
Brigadier General Charles K. Graham

Engineers
Major Joseph Walker
1st New York (8 companies)

Siege Artillery
Colonel Henry L. Abbot
1st Connecticut Heavy Artillery
12th New York Heavy Artillery (companies A and H)
3rd Pennsylvania Heavy Artillery (company M)
Cavalry Division
Brigadier General Augustus V. Kautz

First Brigade
Colonel Simon H. Mix
3rd New York
5th Pennsylvania

Second Brigade
Colonel Samuel P. Spear
1st District of Columbia
11th Pennsylvania

Third Brigade
Colonel Andrew W. Evans
1st Maryland
1st New York Mounted Rifles

Cavalry Division
Brigadier General Ranald S. Mackenzie

First Brigade
Colonel R. M. West
5th Pennsylvania
20th New York (1 company)

Second Brigade
Colonel S. P. Spear
11th Pennsylvania
1st Maryland Cavalry
Battalion First District of Columbia

On December 3, 1864, the XVIII Corps was de-activated. Its white troops went with those of the X Corps to form the new XXIV Corps, and its black troops went with those of the X Corps to form the new XXV Corps.

XXIV ARMY CORPS
Major General E. O. C. Ord (on leave), Brigadier General Alfred H. Terry

Headquarters Guard
8th Connecticut

Provost Guard and Orderlies
Companies F and K, 4th Massachusetts Cavalry (detachments)

First Division
Brigadier General Robert S. Foster

First Brigade
Colonel Thomas O. Osborn
39th Illinois
62nd Ohio
67th Ohio
199th Pennsylvania

Second Brigade
Brigadier General Joseph R. Hawley
6th Connecticut
3rd New Hampshire
7th New Hampshire
6th New York Heavy Artillery (6 companies)

Third Brigade
Colonel Harris M. Plaisted
10th Connecticut
11th Maine
24th Massachusetts
100th New York
206th Pennsylvania

Fourth Brigade
Colonel James Jourdan
8th Maine
89th New York
148th New York
158th New York
55th Pennsylvania

Second Division
Brigadier General Adelbert Ames.

First Brigade
Colonel N. Martin Curtis
3rd New York
112th New York
117th New York
142nd New York

Second Brigade
Colonel Galuslia Pennypacker
47th New York
48th New York
76th Pennsylvania
97th Pennsylvania
203rd Pennsylvania

Third Brigade
Colonel Louis Bell
13th Indiana (5 companies)
9th Maine
4th New Hampshire
115th New York
169th New York

Third Division
Brigadier General Charles Devens, Jr

First Brigade
Lieutenant Colonel John B. Raulston
11th Connecticut
13th New Hampshire
81st New York
98th New York
139th New York
19th Wisconsin

Second Brigade
Colonel Joseph H. Potter
5th Maryland
10th New Hampshire
12th New Hampshire
96th New York
118th New York
9th Vermont

Third Brigade
Colonel Guy V. Henry
21st Connecticut
40th Massachusetts
2nd New Hampshire
58th Pennsylvania
188th Pennsylvania

First Infantry Division (Army of West Virginia)
Colonel Thomas M. Harris
(Temporarily attached to XXIV Corps)

First Brigade
Lieutenant Colonel Thomas F. Wiles
34th Massachusetts
116th Ohio
123rd Ohio

Second Brigade
Colonel William B. Curtis
23rd Illinois (5 companies)
54th Pennsylvania
12th West Virginia

Third Brigade
Colonel Milton Wells
10th West Virginia
11th West Virginia
15th West Virginia

Artillery Brigade
Major Charles C. Abell
Battery E, 3rd New York
Battery H, 3rd New York
Battery K, 3rd New York
Battery M, 3rd New York
7th New York
16th New York
17th New York
A, 1st Pennsylvania
Battery F, 1st Rhode Island
Battery L, 4th US
Battery A, 5th US
Battery F, 5th US

XXV ARMY CORPS
Major General Godfrey Weitzel
(All the infantry were colored troops)

Provost Guard
E and H, 4th Massachusetts Cavalry

First Division
Brigadier General Charles J. Paine

First Brigade
Colonel Delevan Bates
1st US
27th US
30th US

Second Brigade
Colonel John W. Ames
4th US
6th US
39th US

Third Brigade
Colonel Elias Wright
5th US
10th US
37th US
107th US

Second Division
Brigadier General William Birney

First Brigade
Colonel Charles S. Russell
7th US
109th US
116th US
117th US

Second Brigade
Colonel Ulysses Doubleday
8th US
45th US (6 companies)
127th US

Third Brigade
Colonel Henry C. Ward
28th US
29th US
31st US

Third Division
Brigadier General Edward A. Wild

First Brigade
Colonel Alonzo G. Draper
22nd US
36th US
38th US
118th US

Second Brigade
Colonel Edward Martindale
29th Connecticut
9th US
41st US

Third Brigade
Brigadier General Henry G. Thomas
19th US
23rd US
43rd US

Unassigned
2nd US Colored Cavalry (dismounted)

Artillery Brigade
Lieutenant Colonel Richard H. Jackson
1st Connecticut
4th New Jersey
5th New Jersey
16th New York Heavy (detachment)
Battery E, 1st Pennsylvania
Battery C, 3rd Rhode Island
Battery D, 1st US
Battery M, 1st US
Battery E, 3rd US
Battery D, 4th US

Cavalry Division
Brigadier General Augustus V. Kautz

First Brigade
Colonel Robert M. West
5th Pennsylvania, Lt. Col. Christopher Kleinz
3rd New York, Col.
Second Brigade
Colonel Samuel P. Spear
11th Pennsylvania, Lt. Col. Franklin A. Stratton
1st District of Columbia (4 companies), Maj. J. Stannard Baker

Third Brigade
Colonel Andrew W. Evans
1st Maryland, Lieut. Col. Jacob H. Counselman
1st New York Mounted Rifles, Col. Edwin V. Sumner

Artillery
4th Wisconsin, Capt. Dorman L. Noggle
B, 1st US, Lt. Theodore K. Gibbs

Cavalry Division
Brigadier General James H. Wilson

First Brigade
Colonel Timothy M. Bryan, Jr.
1st Connecticut, Maj. Erastus Blakeslee
2nd New York, Col. Otto Harhaus
5th New York, Lt. Col. John Hammond
18th Pennsylvania, Lt. Col. William P. Brinton

Second Brigade
Colonel George H. Chapman
3rd Indiana, Maj. William Patton
8th New York, Lt. Col. William H. Benjamin
1st Vermont, Lt. Col. Addison W. Preston

Cavalry Division
Major General Alfred T. A. Torbert
Brigadier General Wesley Merritt

1st Brigade
Colonel James H. Kidd
1st Michigan Cavalry
5th Michigan Cavalry
6th Michigan Cavalry
7th Michigan Cavalry
6th New York Battery

2nd Brigade
Brigadier General Thomas C. Devin
4th New York Cavalry (Headquarters Guard)
6th New York Cavalry
9th New York Cavalry
19th New York Cavalry
Batteries K and L, 5th US Artillery

ARMY OF THE SHENANDOAH (SHERIDAN'S CAVALRY COMMAND)

Major General Philip H. Sheridan (April 5, 1864–March 25, 1865)
Major General Wesley Merritt (March 25–May 22, 1865)

Escort 1st Rhode Island

First Division
Brigadier General Thomas C. Devin.

First Brigade
Colonel Peter Stagg
1st Michigan
5th Michigan
7th Michigan
6th New York Battery

Second Brigade
Colonel Charles L. Fitzhugh
4th New York
6th New York
9th New York
19th New York (1st Dragoons)
Batteries K and L, 1st US Artillery

Reserve Brigade
Brigadier General Alfred Gibbs
2nd Massachusetts
1st US
5th US
6th US

Second Division
Major General George Crook

First Brigade
Brigadier General Henry E. Davies, Jr
1st Massachusetts
1st New Jersey
10th New York
1st Pennsylvania

Second Brigade
Colonel Samuel B. M. Young
1st Maine
2nd Pennsylvania
4th Pennsylvania

8th Pennsylvania
13th Pennsylvania
16th Pennsylvania

Third Brigade
Brigadier General Charles H. Smith
1st Maine
2nd New York Mounted Rifles
6th Ohio
13th Ohio

Third Division
Brigadier General George A. Custer

First Brigade
Colonel Alexander C. M. Pennington, Jr
1st Connecticut
3rd New Jersey
2nd New York
5th New York
2nd Ohio
18th Pennsylvania

Second Brigade
Colonel William Wells
3rd Indiana (2 companies)
1st New Hampshire (battalion)
8th New York
22nd New York
1st Vermont

Second Brigade
Colonel Henry Capehart
1st New York
1st West Virginia
2nd West Virginia
3rd West Virginia
Battery L, 5th US

Horse Artillery
Batteries B and L, 2nd US
Batteries C, F, and K, 3rd US

ARMY OF NORTHERN VIRGINIA

Approximately 54,750 men
Commander: General Robert E. Lee, General-in-Chief of Confederate Forces

FIRST ARMY CORPS
Lieutenant General James "Old Pete" Longstreet

Pickett's Division
Major General George E. Pickett

Steuart's Brigade
Brigadier General George H. Steuart
9th Virginia
14th Virginia
38th Virginia
53rd Virginia
57th Virginia

Corse's Brigade
Brigadier General Montgomery D. Corse
15th Virginia
17th Virginia
29th Virginia
30th Virginia
32nd Virginia

Hunton's Brigade
Brigadier General Eppa Hunton
8th Virginia
18th Virginia
19th Virginia
28th Virginia
56th Virginia

Mayo's Brigade
Brigadier General William R. Terry/Colonel Joseph Mayo, Jr
1st Virginia
3rd Virginia
7th Virginia
11th Virginia
24th Virginia

Field's Division
Major General Charles W. Field

Anderson's Brigade
Brigadier General George T. Anderson
7th Georgia
8th Georgia
9th Georgia
11th Georgia
59th Georgia

Perry's (Late Law's) Brigade
Brigadier General William F. Perry
4th Alabama
15th Alabama
44th Alabama
47th Alabama
48th Alabama

Gregg's Brigade
Colonel Frederick S. Bass
3rd Arkansas
1st Texas
4th Texas
5th Texas

Benning's Brigade
Brigadier General Henry L. Benning
2nd Georgia
15th Georgia
17th Georgia
20th Georgia

Bratton's Brigade
Brigadier General John Bratton
1st South Carolina
5th South Carolina
6th South Carolina
2nd South Carolina (Rifles)
Palmetto (South Carolina) Sharpshooters

Kershaw's Division
Major General Joseph P. Kershaw

Sanders' Brigade
Brigadier General John C.C. Sanders
16th Georgia
18th Georgia
24th Georgia
3rd Georgia Battalion Sharpshooters
Cobb's (Georgia) Legion
Phillip's (Georgia) Legion

Humphrey's Brigade
Brigadier General B.G. Humphrey
13th Mississippi
17th Mississippi
18th Mississippi
21st Mississippi

Bryan's Brigade
Brigadier General Goode Bryan
10th Georgia
50th Georgia
51st Georgia
53rd Georgia

Connor's Brigade
Brigadier General James Connor
2nd South Carolina
3rd South Carolina
7th South Carolina
8th South Carolina
15th South Carolina
20th South Carolina
3rd South Carolina Battalion

Artillery
Brigadier General Edward P. Alexander

Cabell's Battalion
Colonel Henry C. Cabell
1st Company, Richmond Howitzers (Virginia)
Callaway's Georgia Battery
Troup Artillery (Georgia)
Ellis Light Artillery (North Carolina)

Huger's Battalion
Lieutenant Colonel Frank Huger
Brooks Artillery (South Carolina)
Madison Tipperary's (Louisiana)
Parker Battery (Virginia)
Bedford Light Artillery (Virginia)
Taylor's Virginia Battery
Ashland Artillery (Virginia)

Hardaway's Battalion
Lieutenant Colonel R.A. Hardaway
Powhatan Artillery (Virginia)
Rockbridge Artillery (Virginia)
Salem Flying Artillery (Virginia)
3rd Co., Richmond Howitzers (Virginia)

Haskell's Battalion
Major John C. Haskell
Branch Artillery (North Carolina)
Ramsey's North Carolina Battery
Palmetto Light Battery, 2nd, (South Carolina)
Nelson Light Artillery (Virginia)

Stark's Battalion
Lieutenant Colonel A.W. Stark
Louisiana Guard Battery
Matthews Light Artillery (Virginia)
Giles Light Artillery (Virginia)

SECOND ARMY CORPS
Major General John B. Gordon

Rodes's Division
Major General Robert E. Rodes

Battle's Brigade
Colonel Edwin L. Hobson
3rd Alabama
5th Alabama
6th Alabama
12th Alabama
61st Alabama

Grimes' Brigade
Colonel David G. Cowand
32nd North Carolina
43rd North Carolina
45th North Carolina
53rd North Carolina
2nd North Carolina Battalion

Cox's Brigade
Brigadier General William R. Cox
1st North Carolina
2nd North Carolina
3rd North Carolina
4th North Carolina
14th North Carolina
30th North Carolina

Cook's Brigade
Colonel Edwin A. Nash
4th Georgia
12th Georgia
21st Georgia
44th Georgia
Patterson's Georgia Battery

Archer's Battalion
Lieutenant Colonel Fletcher H. Archer
3rd Battalion Virginia Reserves (Petersburg Reserves)
44th Virginia Battalion

Early's Division
Brigadier General John Pegram/James A. Walker

Johnston's Brigade
Colonel John W. Lea
5th North Carolina
12th North Carolina
20th North Carolina
23rd North Carolina
1st North Carolina Battalion Sharpshooters

Lewis' Brigade
Captain John Beard
6th North Carolina
21st North Carolina
54th North Carolina
57th North Carolina

Pegram's Brigade
Major Henry Kyd Douglas
13th Virginia
31st Virginia
49th Virginia
52nd Virginia
58th Virginia

Gordon's Division
Brigadier General Clement A. Evans

Evan's Brigade
Col. John H. Lowe
13th Georgia
26th Georgia
31st Georgia
38th Georgia
60th and 61st Georgia (consolidated)
9th Georgia Battalion Artillery
12th Georgia Battalion Artillery
18th Georgia Battalion Infantry

Terry's (Stonewall) Brigade
Brigadier General William Terry
2nd Virginia
4th Virginia
5th Virginia
10th Virginia
21st Virginia
23rd Virginia
25th Virginia
27th Virginia
33rd Virginia
37th Virginia
42nd Virginia
44th Virginia
48th Virginia

York's Brigade
Colonel Eugene Waggaman
1st Louisiana
2nd Louisiana
5th Louisiana
6th Louisiana
7th Louisiana
8th Louisiana
9th Louisiana
10th Louisiana
14th Louisiana
15th Louisiana

Artillery
Brigadier General Armistead L. Long

Hardaway's Battalion
Lieutenant Colonel Robert A. Hardaway
Virginia Battery (Powhatan Artillery)
Virginia Battery (Rockbridge Artillery)
Virginia Battery (Salem Flying Artillery)
Virginia Battery (3rd Co., Richmond Howitzers)

Cutshaw's Battalion
Major Wilfred E. Cutshaw
Virginia Battery (Henrico Artillery)
Virginia Battery (Staunton Artillery)
Virginia Battery (Orange Artillery)
Virginia Battery (Morris Artillery)

THIRD ARMY CORPS
Lieutenant General Ambrose P. Hill

Heth's Division
Major General Henry Heth

Davis' Brigade
Brigadier General Joseph R. Davis
2nd Mississippi
11th Mississippi
26th Mississippi
42nd Mississippi
55th North Carolina
1st Confederate Battalion

Cooke's Brigade
Brigadier General John R. Cooke
15th North Carolina
27th North Carolina
46th North Carolina
48th North Carolina
55th North Carolina

MacRae's Brigade
Brigadier General William McRae
11th North Carolina
26th North Carolina
44th North Carolina
47th North Carolina
52nd North Carolina

Archer's Brigade
Colonel Robert M. Mayo
1st Tennessee (Provisional Army)
7th Tennessee
14th Tennessee
13th Alabama

Walker's Brigade
Brigadier General Birkett D. Fry
2nd Maryland Battalion
22nd Virginia Battalion
40th Virginia
55th Virginia

Johnson's Brigade

Colonel John M. Hughs
17th and 23rd Tennessee (consolidated)
25th and 44th Tennessee
63rd Tennessee

Wilcox's Division
Major General Cadmus M. Wilcox

Thomas' Brigade
Brigadier General Edward L. Thomas
14th Georgia
35th Georgia
45th Georgia
49th Georgia

Lane's Brigade
Brigadier General James H. Lane
18th North Carolina
28th North Carolina
33rd North Carolina
37th North Carolina

McGowan's Brigade
Brigadier General Samuel McGowan
1st South Carolina (Provisional Army)
12th South Carolina
13th South Carolina
14th South Carolina
Orr's (South Carolina) Rifles

Scales' Brigade
Brigadier General Alfred M. Scales
13th North Carolina
16th North Carolina
22nd North Carolina
34th North Carolina
38th North Carolina

Mahone's Division
Major General William Mahone

Forney's Brigade
Brigadier General William H. Forney
8th Alabama
9th Alabama
10th Alabama
11th Alabama
13th Alabama
14th Alabama

Weisiger's Brigade
Brigadier General David A. Weisiger
6th Virginia
12th Virginia
16th Virginia
41st Virginia
61st Virginia

Harris' Brigade
Brigadier General Nathaniel H. Harris
12th Mississippi
16th Mississippi
19th Mississippi
48th Mississippi

Wright's Brigade
Colonel George E. Taylor
3rd Georgia
22nd Georgia
48th Georgia
64th Georgia
2nd Georgia Battalion
10th Georgia Battalion

Finegan's Brigade
Colonel David Lang
2nd Florida
5th Florida
8th Florida
9th Florida
10th Florida
11th Florida

Artillery
Colonel R. Lindsay Walker

McIntosh's Battalion
Lieutenant Colonel William M. Owen
Hurt's Alabama Battery
Washington Artillery, 1st Company (Louisiana)
Chesapeake Battery (Maryland)
Davidson's Battery (Virginia)
Danville/Eighth Star Artillery (Virginia)
Rockbridge Artillery No. 2 (Virginia)

Poague's Battalion
Lieutenant Colonel William T. Poague
Madison Light Artillery (Mississippi)
Charlotte Artillery (North Carolina)
Albemarle Artillery (Virginia)
Utterback's Virginia Light Artillery
Penick's Virginia Light Artillery
Otey Battery (Virginia)
Ringgold Battery (Virginia)

Richardson Battalion
Lieutenant Colonel Charles Richardson
Landry's Louisiana Battery
Huger Battery (Virginia)
Norfolk Light Artillery Blues (Virginia)

Pegram's Battalion
Colonel William J. Pegram
McQueen Light Artillery (South Carolina)
Purcell Battery (Virginia)
Crewnshaw's Battery (Virginia)
Letcher Artillery (Virginia)

ANDERSON'S CORPS
Lieutenant General Richard Heron Anderson

Hoke's Division
Major General Robert F. Hoke

Martin's Brigade
Brigadier General James G. Martin
17th North Carolina
42nd North Carolina
66th North Carolina

Clingman's Brigade
Brigadier General Thomas L. Clingman
8th North Carolina
31st North Carolina
51st North Carolina
61st North Carolina

Hagood's Brigade
Brigadier General Johnson Hagood
11th South Carolina
21st South Carolina
25th South Carolina
27th South Carolina

Colquitt's Brigade
Brigadier General Alfred H. Colquitt
6th Georgia
19th Georgia
23rd Georgia
27th Georgia
28th Georgia

28th Virginia Artillery Battalion
Major John P.W. Read
Blount's Virginia Battery
Caskie's Virginia Battery
Macon's Virginia Battery
Marshall's Virginia Battery

Johnson's Division
Major General Bushrod R. Johnson

Wise's Brigade
Brigadier General Henry A. Wise
26th Virginia
34th Virginia
46th Virginia
59th Virginia

Wallace's Brigade
Colonel William H. Wallace
17th South Carolina
18th South Carolina
22nd South Carolina
23rd South Carolina
26th South Carolina
Holcombe (South Carolina) Legion

Moody's Brigade
Brigadier General Young M. Moody
41st Alabama
43rd Alabama
59th Alabama
60th Alabama
23rd Alabama Battalion

Ransom's Brigade
Colonel Lee McAfee
24th North Carolina
25th North Carolina
35th North Carolina
49th North Carolina
56th North Carolina

Artillery
Colonel Hilary P. Jones

Blount's Battalion
Macon Light Artillery (Georgia)
Cape Fear Light Artillery (North Carolina)
Miller's Battery (North Carolina)
Halifax Light Artillery (Virginia)

Stribling's Battalion
Blount's Virginia Battery
Marshall's Virginia Battery
Macon's Virginia Battery
Sullivan's Virginia Battery

Coit's Battalion
Major James C. Coit
Mississippi Battery (Bradford's)
Branch Field Artillery (Virginia)
Wright's Virginia Battery

Smith's Battalion
Captain William F. Dement
1st Maryland Battery
Johnston's Virginia Battery
Neblett's Heavy Artillery (Virginia)
Drewry's Artillery (Virginia)
Kevill's Battery (Virginia)

CAVALRY CORPS
Major General Wade Hampton

Butler's Division
Major General M.C. Butler

Butler's Brigade
Colonel H. K. Aiken
4th South Carolina
5th South Carolina
6th South Carolina

Young's Brigade
Colonel J. F. Waring
10th Georgia
Cobb's Georgia Legion
Phillips Georgia Legion
Jeff. Davis Mississippi Legion

Lee's Division
Major General W. H. F. Lee.

Barringer's Brigade
Brigadier General Rufus Barringer
1st North Carolina
2nd North Carolina
3rd North Carolina
5th North Carolina

Beale's Brigade
Brigadier General R. L. T. Beale (Brigadier General John R. Chambliss, Jr)
9th Virginia
10th Virginia
13th Virginia

Dearing's Brigade
Brigadier General James Dearing
8th Georgia
4th North Carolina
12th North Carolina Battalion
16th North Carolina Battalion

Fitzhugh Lee's Division
Major General Fitzhugh Lee

Wickham's Brigade
Brigadier General Williams C. Wickham
1st Virginia
2nd Virginia
3rd Virginia
4th Virginia

Rosser's Brigade
Brigadier General Thomas L. Rosser
7th Virginia
11th Virginia
12th Virginia
35th Virginia Battalion

Payne's Brigade
Brigadier General William H.F. Payne
5th Virginia
6th Virginia
15th Virginia

Horse Artillery
Major R. Preston Chew
South Carolina Battery (Hart's)
Graham's Virginia Battery
McGregor's Virginia Battery.

BIBLIOGRAPHY

Bearss, E. and C. Calkins, *Battle of Five Forks* (Lynchburg, VA: H.E. Howard, 1985)

Brinton, J.H., *Personal Memoirs of John H. Brinton, Major and Surgeon U.S.V., 1861–1865* (New York: Neale Publishing Co., 1914)

Caldwell, J.F.J., *History of a Brigade of South Carolinians* (Philadelphia, PA: 1866)

Cannan, J., *The Crater: Burnside's Assault on the Confederate Trenches, June 30, 1864* (Da Capo Press: Cambridge, MA, 2002)

Cavanaugh, M. and W. Marvel, *The Petersburg Campaign:"The Horrid Pit," Battle of the Crater: June 25–August 6, 1864* (Lynchburg, VA: H.E. Howard, 1989)

Clark, J. H., *The Iron Hearted Regiment: Being an Account of the Battles, Marches and Deeds Performed by the 115th Regiment N.Y. Volunteers* (Albany, NY: 1865)

Etheredge, W.H., "Another Story of the Crater Battle," *Southern Historical Society Papers*, (Richmond, VA, January–December 1909), Vol. XXXVII

Featherston, J.C., "Graphic Account of the Battle of the Crater," *Southern Historical Society Papers* (Richmond, VA, January–December 1905), Vol. XXXIII

Field, R., *American Civil War Fortifications (2) Land and field fortifications* (Oxford, UK: 2005)

Freeman, D.S., *R.E. Lee: A Biography*, 4 vols. (New York: Charles Scribner's Sons, 1935)

Friend, A., *Memorial of Colonel John A. Bross, Twenty-ninth U.S. Colored Troops* (Chicago, Illinois: Tribune Book and Job Office, 1865)

Greene, A.W., *Breaking the Backbone of the Rebellion: The Final Battles of the Petersburg Campaign* (Mason City, Iowa: Savas Publishing Company, 2000)

Greene, A.W., *Civil War Petersburg: Confederate City in the Crucible of War* (Charlottesville, VA: University of Virginia Press, 2006)

Gould, J., *The Story of the Forty-Eighth: A Record of the Campaigns of the Forty-Eighth Regiment Pennsylvania Volunteer Infantry During the Four Eventful Years of Its Service In the War for the Preservation of the Union* (Philadelphia, Pennsylvania: 1908)

Hewett, J.B. (ed.), *Supplement to the Official Records of the Union and Confederate Armies* (Wilmington, NC: Broadfoot Publishing Company, 1994–2001)

Johnson, R.U. and C.C. Buel, *Battles and Leaders of the Civil War*, 4 vols. (New York: The Century Co., 1887–88)

Marshall, J.A., *Private and Official Correspondence of Gen. Benjamin F. Butler, During the Period of the Civil War*, 4 vols. (Norwood, MA: Plimpton Press, 1917)

McMaster, F.W., "The Battle of the Crater, July 30, 1864," *Southern Historical Society Papers* (Richmond, VA, March 1882), Vol. X. No. 3

McMurray, J., *Recollections of a Colored Troop* (Brookville, PA: McMurray Co., 1994)

Scott, R.N. (ed.), *The War of the Rebellion: A Compilation of the Official Records of the Union and Confederate Armies* (Washington, DC: 1880–1901)

Trudeau, N.A., *The Last Citadel: Petersburg, Virginia, June 1864–April 1865* (Baton Rouge, LA: Louisiana State University Press, 1993)

Various newspapers and journals

INDEX

References to illustrations are shown in **bold**. Plates are prefixed pl, with captions on the page in brackets.